FOLK SONGS OF
THE AMERICAS

FOLK SONGS OF THE AMERICAS

edited by

A. L. Lloyd

for the

INTERNATIONAL FOLK MUSIC COUNCIL

Associate Editor

Isabel Aretz de Ramón y Rivera

Prepared under the auspices
of the
INTERNATIONAL MUSIC COUNCIL
with the assistance of the
UNITED NATIONS EDUCATIONAL, SCIENTIFIC AND
CULTURAL ORGANISATION (UNESCO)

Amsco Music Publishing Company
799 Broadway, New York City, N.Y. 10003
International Copyright Secured
All Rights Reserved

Lithographed in U.S.A. by

EDWARDS
BROTHERS
INCORPORATED

2500 SOUTH STATE STREET / ANN ARBOR, MICHIGAN 48104

First published 1965

This edition published 1966 by special
arrangement with the original publisher,
Novello and Company Limited, London.

FOREWORD

THE traverse from the snows of Canada to the squalls of Patagonia passes through many climates with diverse human conditions and a protean array of cultures. To attempt to contain within a modest-sized book even a sampling of the many folk song traditions to be encountered on the long journey, is a task that has caused wiser men than the present Editor to quail. Roughly, the songs in this book belong to three great areas of musical culture. First is the North American area, having European-based melody, though with a powerful Negro addition in its southern region. Next is the so-called Antillean area (though its influence extends at least as far south as Rio), in which the music is part-European, part-African. Third is the Andean area (again, the name is misleading, for the territory stretches to the River Plate) where the melodic repertory is made up of varying mixtures of European and Indian elements. Not all the regions within those areas have been well served by folk music collectors; and where collections have been made they have not always been readily accessible to us. Thus, the selection of folk songs of the Americas offered here has regrettable shortcomings and actual gaps, but it is hoped that readers may gain from it some idea of the kind of songs that common folk have made for themselves to sing in the woods of Quebec, among the laurels of Kentucky, in the Caribbean canefields and the fazendas of Brazil, amid the rigours of the Andes and on the cattle-plains of the pampa. Further, we trust that many will be encouraged to sing the songs, even though some may come from remote traditions formed from ways of life obscure to most of us.

Songs of the remotest traditions of all, of the Eskimos, North American Indians, and aboriginal peoples of the Latin American hinterland, do not appear here. Such items of musical ethnography are, perhaps, out of place in a song book intended for general popular use. We have limited our selection to songs made on European pattern, or to Negro-European or Indian-European hybrids of reasonably manageable character. Many of the pieces here are of easy charm, and those of tarter flavour are generally picturesque enough to be agreeable. We take this to be fitting for a book meant for the entertainment of non-specialist readers and singers.

Even so, some items in our selection offer a stern challenge to all but the boldest performers. It is the fact that some of the most important song-types in the traditions of the Americas do not conform to the neatly-architected, easily-contained patterns that are dominant in European song. Nor are the beauties always so readily apparent from a more-or-less skeletal notation. Moreover, the deep sense of certain pieces is hard to grasp and harder to express. Thus, for instance, the United States blues, the Venezuelan polo, the Argentine baguala, are types of tremendous power in their respective traditions, and to omit them from a sampling of American songs would be 'perverse and foolish' indeed. Yet each, in its different way, defies

v

convincing performance by outsiders unless they be of the most judicious. The bahuala seems too simple, the polo too complicated, and a clear view of the blues is obscured by clouds of prejudice and over-enthusiasm. More important, the part that these songs play in the lives of their authentic bearers is so intimate that it seems presumptuous for the outsider to attempt to reproduce them without special knowledge and affection. Yet it cannot be denied that these pieces earn their place, and honourably, in such a book as this (see Nos. 58, 124, 152).

A word of explanation is due to readers unfamiliar with Latin American traditions. In some regions, particularly in Mexico, Cuba, and along the east coast of South America, there has for long been enthusiastic give-and-take between town music and country music, with the result that folk music has become so saturated with factors from popular music, and popular music so permeated with folk song elements, that the two are often barely distinguishable, and that elusive abstraction called 'authentic folk song' is hardly to be found, though country populations may be leading musical lives of great vigour, based on songs mainly created by themselves. This cultural exchange between the world of books and the world of orality shows in texts no less than in tunes. Thus, the unlettered Margarita Island fishermen who sing our example No. 124 find nothing untoward in expressing their feelings about the mystery of night in such literary terms as: 'Mi ánima sutil nunca se sacia/de gustar su inefable poesía/ y encarecer su excelsa aristocracia' (literally: My subtle mind is never sated with savouring its ineffable poetry and extolling its lofty aristocracy). Inevitably then, many examples in this book are the products of a syncretism that sometimes disturbs the folklorist but seldom dismays the folk.

In preparing this book, we have been given pause by the problem of accompanied folk song. Unlike Europe, where folk song is generally (though by no means exclusively) unaccompanied, America presents a whole parade of folk song types in which accompaniment is an essential traditional feature. This is notably the case with Latin American dance songs, an important class whose melodies are quite frequently of little meaning without the accompaniment of guitar, cuatro, tiple, charango, rattle, drum. Many a melody in the Antillean-Brazilian complex looks very thin in its three-four notation, but how it springs to fullness when set against its six-eight accompaniment! And what is a polo, a cueca, a chacarera, a gato, without at least some indication of the instrumental support that traditionally belongs to it? So in a number of cases, with Latin American tunes, we have given a sketch of how the song is accompanied by traditional performers (this has not been attempted with examples from North America, since folklorists there have generally been content to notate the melody only, and scientifically-made transcriptions of the accompaniments—where they occur in traditional performance —are hard to seek). In a few instances, where the song in its natural state is sung polyphonically, we have provided the parts, which are, as a rule, of the simplest.

English translations have been provided for the songs. Here too, a note of explanation is called for. Particularly in Latin American dance songs, the sense of the text is often of scant importance; what matters is the rumbling rhythm of the words. Those Iberian reverberations are hard to reproduce in English, and the difficulty is added to by the habit—again commonest in the Negro-influenced music of the Antillean-Brazilian area—of adding spice to the song by stressing unimportant words and weak syllables. In Trinidad, the matter is expressed thus:

> If you want to sing calypSO, you got to be able
> Always put the acCENT on the wrong syllAYble.

Of course, it must be the right 'wrong' syllable that is accented, or the result is unsingable. Generally the translators of the songs in this book have provided versions that fit the melody in the normal way. But, with the Latin American songs, the best of translations cannot equal the original text in aptitude, and the translators would join the Editors in imploring those who wish to sing the songs with Spanish or Portuguese texts to ignore the English versions and to use the original language wherever possible. To help those who are not linguists, a Guide to Spanish Pronunciation is provided on page xvii.

The Council is grateful to all who helped to prepare this book; to publishers and copyright owners who gave permission to print the songs; and to the translators whose names appear on page ix, and the Editor is pleased to take this opportunity to insert a special word of thanks to his Associate, Señora Isabel Aretz de Ramón y Rivera, who provided the greater part of the Latin American material, much of it from her matchless personal collection. Without her help, the preparation of this book would hardly have been possible.

A. L. L.

ACKNOWLEDGEMENTS

Permission to use existing copyright material has been granted by the following copyright owners:

M. Barbeau	1, 3, 5, 6, 7, 8, 9, 11
Columbia Records Inc., and Alan Lomax	.. 10
Harvard University Press	.. 13, 15, 20, 24, 34, 35, 50, 51
Oxford University Press and Maud Karpeles	14, 16, 18, 19, 22, 25, 31–33, 36, 37, 39–44, 49
National Museum of Canada and M. Barbeau	17, 23
Dr Helen Creighton and The Ryerson Press, Toronto ..	.. 21
Essex Music, Ltd.	30, 38, 45, 47, 54, 56, 81
American Folklore Society	26, 80
Moses Asch, Folkways Records and Service Corp.	27, 46
University of Pennsylvania Press	.. 28
Yale University and Mrs Marston	.. 29
Sing Out, Inc.	.. 48
Routledge and Kegan Paul Ltd.	.. 53
University of Alabama Press	.. 60
Vincente T. Mendoza and Instituto de Investigaciones Estéticas ..	64–70
Pan-American Union	.. 71–75, 78, 79
Director of Folklore Nacional de Honduras	73–75
Ministry of Education, Costa Rica	76, 77
Fernando Ortiz	.. 82
H. Courlander and The University of California Press ..	88, 89
J. D. Elder	94–99
Abelardo Gutiérrez	100–104
O. Alvarenga	115–121
R. and M. d'Harcourt	122–125
Maria Luisa Escobar	.. 113
Isabel Aretz de Ramón y Rivera	106–7, 126–135, 137–150

We are indebted to the following for the use of the following material in the public domain but taken from their collections;

Library of Congress	.. 52
Albert and Charles Boni Inc.	62, 63
Maria Luisa Escobar	.. 108

Every effort has been made to obtain permission for the use of copyright material in this book. The Council and Publishers ask forgiveness if through inadvertance any copyright material has been printed without permission.

COLLECTORS

A. L. ..	..	Argeliers León
A. L. (a)	..	Alan Lomax
B. A. ..	..	Byron Arnold
B. A. B.	..	B. A. Botkin
B. A. G.	..	Benigno A. Gutierrez
C. J. S...	..	Cecil J. Sharp
C. L. E.	..	C. L. Edwards
C. M. ..	..	Concha Michel
C. V. ..	..	Carlos Vega
E. B. G.	..	Elisabeth Bristol Greenleaf
E. G. ..	..	Ernest Gagnon
E. Y. H.	..	E. Y. Harburg
F. C. ..	..	F. Carreño
F. R. ..	..	Franz Rickaby
G. A. ..	..	Graciela Amador
G. Y. M.	..	Grace Yarrow Mansfield
H. C. ..	..	Harold Courlander
H. M. B.	..	H. M. Belden
I. A. ..	..	Isabel Aretz
J. A. L.	..	John A. Lomax
J. C. ..	..	Josiah Combs
J. D. E.	..	J. D. Elder
J. L. ..	..	Juan Liscano
L. F. R. y R.	..	Luis F. Ramón y Rivera
M. B. ..	..	Marius Barbeau
M. d'H.	..	Marguérite d'Harcourt
M. K. ..	..	Maud Karpeles
M. O...	..	Martin Osorio
M. T. L.	..	María Teresa Linares
P. B. ..	..	Phillips Barry
R. A. D.	..	R. Aristóbulo Dominguez
R. E. K.	..	Robert E. Kennedy
R. d'H.	..	Raoul d'Harcourt
R. M. ..	..	Rafael Manzanares
R. P. B.	..	R. P. Benitez
S. M. ..	..	Susana Mendoza
S. P. B.	..	Samuel P. Bayard
V. R. ..	..	Vance Randolph
V. R. R. M.	..	Virginia Rodríguez Rivera de Mendoza
V. T. M.	..	Vicente T. Mendoza
W. J. ..	..	Walter Jekyll
W. R. McK.	..	W. Roy McKenzie
Z. N. H.	..	Zora N. Hurston

TRANSLATORS

A. L. L. ..	..	A. L. Lloyd
M. K. ..	..	Maud Karpeles
N. F. ..	..	Norman Fraser
V. K. ..	..	Victoria Kingsley
V. M. ..	..	Vincent Morley

CONTENTS

page

Foreword v
Acknowledgements viii
Collectors ix
Translators ix
Sources of the Songs xiv
A Guide to Spanish Pronunciation xvii

CANADA:
1 Renaud 2
2 Isabeau s'y promène 4
3 Blanche comme la neige 6
4 Quand j'étais chez mon père 8
5 La Sainte Vierge aux Cheveux Pendants 10
6 Le long de la mer jolie 12
7 Dans les Haubans 14
8 J'ai cueilli la belle rose 16
9 Là-haut sur ces montagnes 18
10 En roulant ma boule 20
11 Lisette 22
12 Dans les chantiers nous hivernerons 24
13 The Bonny Banks of the Virgie O 26
14 The Lover's Ghost 27
15 Oh, who is at my bedroom window? 28
16 The Gypsy Laddie 29
17 The False Young Man 30
18 The Maid on the Shore 32
19 The Maiden's Lament 34
20 Bold Wolfe 36
21 The Stormy Scenes of Winter 38
22 She's like the swallow 39
23 Mary Ann 40
24 The Lumber Camp Song 42

UNITED STATES OF AMERICA:
25 The Wife of Usher's Well 46
26 Little Matthy Groves 48
27 The House Carpenter 50
28 Mr Woodbury's Courtship 52
29 The Gallows Tree 54
30 The Low-Down Lonesome Low 56
31 Locks and Bolts 58
32 The Nightingale 59
33 Jackie Frazier 60
34 Daniel Monroe 62
35 The Pinery Boy 64

36	The Dear Companion	..	..	..	..	..	65
37	Black is the colour	..	..	..	..	..	66
38	When first to this country a stranger I came	..	..	..	67
39	Every night when the sun goes in	..	..	..	..	68
40	Pretty Saro	..	..	..	..	..	69
41	The chickens they are crowing	..	..	..	..	70
42	Sally Buck	..	..	..	..	..	71
43	Swing a lady round	..	..	..	..	..	72
44	Liza Anne	..	..	..	..	..	73
45	Mamma's gone to the mail boat	..	..	..	..	74
46	The Lazy Farmer	..	..	..	..	..	75
47	Ox-Driving Song	..	..	..	..	..	76
48	The Buffalo Skinners	..	..	..	..	..	78
49	The Dying Cowboy	..	..	..	..	..	80
50	Red Iron Ore	..	..	..	..	..	82
51	A Shanty-Man's Life	..	..	..	..	..	84
52	The Grey Goose	..	..	..	..	..	85
53	Mule on the Mount	..	..	..	..	..	86
54	Lynchburg Town	..	..	..	..	..	87
55	The Babe of Bethlehem	..	..	..	..	..	88
56	Tone the bell easy	..	..	..	..	..	90
57	Gideon's Band	..	..	..	..	..	92
58	Lay dis body down	..	..	..	..	..	94
59	I'll hear the trumpet sound	..	..	..	..	95
60	Tell all the world, John	..	..	..	..	..	96
61	Put John on the islan'	..	..	..	..	..	97
62	Go down, Death	..	..	..	..	..	98
63	Dry Bones	..	..	..	..	..	100

MEXICO:
64	Señora Santa Ana (Lullaby)	..	..	..	..	104
65	Miren cuántas luces (Caminata)	..	..	..	..	106
66	El cura no va a la iglesia (Tonadilla)	..	..	..	108
67	Malhaya la cocina (Tonadilla)	..	..	..	..	111
68	El Matrimonio Desigual (Tonadilla)	..	..	..	..	112
69	Las olas de la laguna (Son)	..	..	..	..	114
70	Cajeme (Corrido)	..	..	..	..	..	116

GUATEMALA:
| 71 | Nací en la cumbre | .. | .. | .. | .. | .. | 118 |
| 72 | Vamos a la mar | .. | .. | .. | .. | .. | 119 |

HONDURAS:
73	Flores de Mimé	..	..	..	..	..	122
74	El Sapo	..	..	..	..	..	124
75	Papanulan	..	..	..	..	..	126

COSTA RICA:
| 76 | El Toro Pinto | .. | .. | .. | .. | .. | 128 |
| 77 | ¡Ay! tituy | .. | .. | .. | .. | .. | 130 |

PANAMA:
| 78 | Hojita de Guarumal | .. | .. | .. | .. | .. | 134 |
| 79 | Mi pollera | .. | .. | .. | .. | .. | 135 |

BAHAMAS:

80 Dig my grave long an' narrow 138
81 The wind blow east 139

CUBA:

82 Má Teodora (Son) 142
83 Yo quisiera vivir en la Habana (Habanera antigua) 144
84 Vamos a hacer un ajiaco (Guaracha antigua) 146
85 Al amanecer del día (Tonada campesina) 147
86 Para los caficultores 148
87 Hay aquí, madre, un jardín 149

HAITI:

88 For Atti Daï (Cult Song) 152
89 Jéorico 154

JAMAICA:

90 Oh, Selina (Digging Song) 158
91 John Thomas (Digging Song) 160
92 Three acre o' coffee (Digging Song) 162
93 Once I was a trav'ller 163

TRINIDAD AND TOBAGO:

94 Anansi, play for Ma Dogoma (Bongo Dance-Song) 166
95 Wind'ard Car'line (Reel Dance-Song) 167
96 Dandy man, oh 168
97 Leggo me han' (Kalinda) 169
98 Cap'n Baker (Kalinda) 170
99 Emma 171

COLOMBIA:

100 El Zancudo 174
101 El Pajarillo 176
102 La Cartagena 177
103 Mi Compadre Mono 178
104 Van cantando por la sierra 180

VENEZUELA:

105 Adorar al niño (Villancico) 182
106 La Corona 184
107 Tono de Velorio de Cruz 186
108 La Burriquita 188
109 El Mampulorio 190
110 Amalia Rosa (Golpe) 192
111 Se fué volando (Fulía) 194
112 Sanguéo 195
113 El Carite 196
114 Que el cantar tiene sentido (Polo Margariteño) 198

BRAZIL:

115 La Na Catarineta (Romance) 202
116 Como pode vivir o peixe (Coreto) 204
117 Tenho um vestido novo (Fandango) 206
118 Da Bahia me mandaram (Coco) 208

xii

119 Triste vida é do marujo 210
120 Vem cá, Cabeleira (Romance) 212
121 Colônia, usina Catende 214

ECUADOR:
122 Yo soy indiecito (Canción Religiosa) 218
123 San Juanito 219
124 Kurikinga (Baile) 220
125 Pirusa 222

PERU:
126 Hakumamai purisisun (Canción Religiosa) 224
127 Dime, lluvia, si ya se divisan 225
128 Al canto de una laguna (Huaino) 226
129 La Lluvia (Huaino) 228
130 El Puquito 230

BOLIVIA:
131 Canto para Cosechar la Papa (Potato-Gathering Song) 232
132 Navidava puri nihua (Villancico) 233
133 Taquircapuscaiqui ari (Huaino) 234
134 He venido, palomita (Huainito) 235

CHILE:
135 Ha nacido en un portal (Esquinazo al Niño Dios) 238
136 La Pastora 240
137 Déjenme paso que voy (Cueca) 242
138 Ingrato, ya no me quieres (Tonada) 245
139 En la cordillera llueve (Cueca) 247

PARAGUAY:
140 La Guaireñita 252
141 Che lucero Aguai-î (Polca Paraguaya) 254

ARGENTINA:
142 Yo no canto por cantar (Baguala salteña) 258
143 Despierta mi palomita (Carnavalito) 260
144 Ahora voy a cantarles (Carnaval de Tilcara) 262
145 Cansado estoy de vivir (Vidala) 263
146 Una palomita (Vidalita) 264
147 Pues que es lo que me dices (Chacarera) 265
148 Dicen que no me quiere (Gato) 266
149 Dicen que las heladas (Cueca) 268

URUGUAY:
150 La terrible inmensidad (Estilo) 272

Index of Songs 275

SOURCES OF SONGS

CANADA

1 *Romancero du Canada.* M. Barbeau. (Toronto: Macmillan, 1937).
2 *Chansons Populaires du Canada.* E. Gagnon. (Montreal: Beauchemin, 1865).
3 *Folk Songs of French Canada.* M. Barbeau and E. Sapir. (New Haven, Conn.: Yale U. Press, 1925).
4 See No. 2.
5, 6 See No. 1.
7 *Folk Songs of Old Quebec.* (Ottawa: National Museum of Canada, n. d.).
8, 9 See No. 1.
10 Transcribed from record *No. SL 211, Columbia World Library of Recorded Folk and Primitive Music, vol. VIII., Canada.* Text completed from Gagnon, *Chansons Populaires du Canada.*
11 See No. 1.
12 See No. 2.
13 *Ballads and Sea Songs of Newfoundland.* E. B. Greenleaf and G. Y. Mansfield. (Cambridge, Mass.: Harvard U. Press, 1933).
14 *Folk Songs from Newfoundland.* M. Karpeles. (London: Oxford U. Press, 1935).
15 *Ballads and Sea Songs from Nova Scotia.* W. R. McKenzie. (Cambridge, Mass.: Harvard U. Press, 1928).
16 See No. 14.
17 National Museum of Canada.
18, 19 See No. 14.
20 See No. 13.
21 *Traditional Songs from Nova Scotia.* H. Creighton and D. H. Senior. (Toronto: The Ryerson Press, 1950).
22 See No. 14.
23 See No. 17.
24 See No. 13.

UNITED STATES OF AMERICA

25 *English Folk Songs from the Southern Appalachians.* C. J. Sharp. (London: Oxford U. Press, 1932).
26 *Journal of American Folklore.* (Boston and New York: American Folklore Society, vol. XXX).
27 Transcribed from record *No. FP 251-A.* (New York: Folkways Records and Service Corp.).
28 *Pennsylvania Songs and Legends.* George Korson (ed.). (Philadelphia: U. of Pennsylvania Press, 1949).
29 *British Ballads from Maine.* P. Barry, F. H. Eckstorm and M. W. Smyth. (New Haven: Yale U. Press, 1929).
30 *Our Singing Country.* J. A. and A. Lomax. (New York: The Macmillan Co., 1941).
31–33 See No. 25.
34 Tune from *Ballads and Songs of the Shanty-Boy.* F. Rickaby. (Cambridge, Mass.: Harvard U. Press, 1926). Text amended from McKenzie and others.
35 *Ballads and Songs of the Shanty-Boy.* F. Rickaby.
36, 37 See No. 25.
38 See No. 30.
39–44 See No. 25.
45 See No. 30.

46 Transcribed from record *No. FP 251-B.* See No. 29.

47 See No. 30.

48 *Sing Out.* (New York: Sing Out Inc., 1956).

49 Melody from Sharp, *English Folk Songs from the Southern Appalachians.* Text amplified from Randolph, Ozark Folksongs, and other sources.

50, 51 See No. 35.

52 Transcribed from record *No. AAFS 15-A, Archive of American Folk Song.* (Washington, D.C.: Library of Congress, 1942).

53 *Mules and Men.* Z. N. Hurston. (London: Kegan Paul, Trench, Trubner & Co. Ltd., 1936).

54 See No. 30.

55 *The Southern Harmony and Musical Companion.* (Philadelphia: E. W. Miller, 1854).

56 *American Ballads and Folk Songs.* J. A. and A. Lomax. (New York: The Macmillan Co., 1934).

57 *Religious Folk Songs of the Negro.* T. P. Fenner. (Hampton, Va.: The Institute Press, 1874).

58 *Slave Songs of the United States.* W. F. Allen. (New York: A. Simpson, 1867).

59 *The Story of the Jubilee Singers.* (London: Hodder & Stoughton, 1876).

60 *Folksongs of Alabama.* B. Arnold. (University, Ala.: U. of Alabama Press, 1950).

61 See No. 57.

62, 63 *Mellows.* R. E. Kennedy. (New York: A. & C. Boni, 1925).

MEXICO

64–70 *Panorama de la Música Tradicional de Mexico.* V. T. Mendoza. (Mexico City: Imprenta Universitaria, 1956).

GUATEMALA

71, 72 Communicated by Music Division, Pan-American Union, Washington, D.C.

HONDURAS

73–75 *Canciones de Honduras.* (Washington, D.C.: Union Panamericana, 1960).

COSTA RICA

76 *Colección de Bailes Tipicos de la Provincia de Guanacaste.* (San José: Secretaria de Educación, 1929).

77 *Colección de Canciones y Danzas Tipicas.* (San José: Secretaria de Educación, 1934).

PANAMA

78, 79 Communicated by Music Division, Pan-American Union, Washington, D.C.

BAHAMAS

80 *Bahama Songs and Stories.* C. L. Edwards. (Boston: American Folklore Society, 1895).

81 See No. 31.

CUBA

82 *La Africania de la Música Popular Cubana.* F. Ortiz. (La Habana: Cardonas, 1950).

83 Communicated by Argeliers León.

84 *El Patrimio Folklérico Musical Cubano.* A. León. (La Habana, 1952).

85–87 See No. 91.

HAITI

88, 89 *The Drum and the Hoe.* H. Courlander. (Berkeley: U. of California Press, 1960).

JAMAICA

90–93 *Jamaican Song and Story*. W. Jekyll. (London: D. Nutt, 1907).

TRINIDAD AND TOBAGO

94–99 Collected and communicated by J. D. Elder.

COLOMBIA

100–104 *Contribución al Estudio del Folklore de Antioquia y Caldas*. B. A. Gutiérrez. (Medellín: Gutiérrez, 1950).

VENEZUELA

105 Collected and transcribed by L. F. Ramón y Rivera.
106, 107 Collected and transcribed by I. Aretz and L. F. Ramón y Rivera.
108 Collected and transcribed by F. Carreño.
109–111 Collected by J. Liscano. Transcribed by L. F. Ramón y Rivera.
112 Collected and transcribed by L. F. Ramón y Rivera.
113 Collected and transcribed by F. Carreño.
114 Collected by J. Liscano. Transcribed by L. F. Ramón y Rivera.
   All the above items from the collection of the Instituto de Folklore, Caracas, Venezuela.

BRAZIL

115–121 *Música Popular Brasileña*. O. Alvarenga. (Mexico City: Fondo de Cultura Economica, 1947).

ECUADOR

122–125 *La Musique des Incas et ses Survivances*. R. and M. d'Harcourt. (Paris: 1925).

PERU

126–130 Collected and transcribed by I. Aretz.

BOLIVIA

131–134 Collected and transcribed by I. Aretz.

CHILE

135,
137–139 Collected and transcribed by I. Aretz.
   136 Transcribed from *RCA Victor record No. CX 20A*. Transcription by Jorge Urrutia Blondel.

   140 Collected by R. Aristóbulo Dominguez. Transcribed by José de J. Villalba.
   141 Collected by I. Aretz and C. Vega. Transcribed by I. Aretz.

ARGENTINA

142–149 Collected and transcribed by I. Aretz.

URUGUAY

150 Collected and transcribed by I. Aretz.

A GUIDE TO SPANISH PRONUNCIATION

Of necessity, this guide is very rough. In Latin America, the pronunciation of Spanish varies from region to region, and Castillian usages can hardly be taken as the absolute standard. Still, the following suggestions may be found useful by those who do not know Spanish, but would like to sing in it.

In spoken Spanish, a word has as many syllables as it has single vowels (Ma-ga-lla-nes) or diphthongs (Bue-nos Ai-res). In sung Spanish, where one vowel-sound follows another, elision is the general rule. Thus 'solita en los campos', 'me has acompañado', 'aquí está el cigarro', are likely to be sung rather as 'solit' en los campos', 'm'as acompañado', 'aquí 'stá'l cigarro'.

Vowels and diphthongs	Sound in Spanish	Vowels and diphthongs	Sound in Spanish
a	a in father	ia	ya in yard
e	a in mate	io	yo in yodel
i	e in mete	ie	yea
o	o in mote	iu	you
u	oo in moot	oi	oy in boy

(*u* after *q* is silent before *e* and *i*, unless it has a diaresis – ü – in which case it is pronounced like *w*).

		ou	oh-oo (run together)
		ua	wah
		ue	way
ai	i in mite	ui	we
au	ow in dowry	uo	woe
ei	ay in may		
eu	ay-oo (run together)		

(*y* used as a vowel is equivalent to the Spanish *i*).

Consonants

b is often an ambiguous, rather *v*-like sound.
c is like *k* before a, o and u.
c is like *s* before e and i (the Castillian 'th' sound for c is not usual in Latin America).
ch is like ch in church.
g is like *g* in go, before a, o and u.
g is like *ch* in loch, before e and i.
h is silent (with rare exceptions)
j is like *ch* in loch.
z is like *s* (again, the Castillian 'lisp' is not usual in Latin America).
ll in Latin America is usually pronounced rather like the *y* in yap, though in some regions it emerges almost like *zh*.
ñ is like *ny* in lanyard.
qu is like *k*.

Stress

When a word ends in a vowel, in *n* or in *s*, the stress falls on the syllable before the last, as balada, cantaban, cantadores.

When a word ends in a consonant other than *n* or *s*, the stress falls on the last syllable, as popular, regional.

However, these rules do not apply when there is a written or printed accent, as canción folklórico de Tánger.

Some Pointers to Portuguese

Portuguese, the language of Brazil, shares most of the Spanish vowel and consonant sounds, though it also includes a number of nasal sounds not heard in Spanish. In Portuguese, *j* has a *zh* sound, like the *s* in leisure; *lh* is like the Spanish *ll*, and *nh* is equivalent to the Spanish *ñ*.

CANADA

1 RENAUD

La mer' é - tant dans les cré - neaux a — vu ve -
nir_ son fils_ Re - naud, Mon fils Re - naud, mon fils ché -
ri, Ta femm' est ac - cou - ché' d'un fils._____

1 La mér' étant dans les créneaux
  A vu venir son fils Renaud.
  – Mon fils Renaud, mon fils chéri,
  Ta femm' est accouché' d'un fils.

2 – Ni de ma femm' ni de mon fils
  Je n'ai le coeur réjoui.
  Je tiens mes trip's et mes boyaux
  Par devant moi dans mon manteau.

3 Ma bonne mèr', entrez devant.
  Faites-moi faire un beau lit blanc.
  Qu'il soit bien fait de point en point,
  Et que ma femm' n'en sache rien.

4 Mais quand ça vint sur le minuit,
  Le beau Renard rendit l'esprit.
  Les servant's s'en vont pleurant
  Et les valets en soupirant.

5 Ah, dites-moi, ma mèr' ô grand',
  Qu'ont les servant's à pleurer tant?
  – C'est la vaissell' qu'elles ont lavé',
  Un beau plat d'or ont égaré.

6 – Pour un plat d'or qu'est egaré
  A quoi sert-il de tant pleurer?
  Quand Renaud de guerre viendra,
  Un beau plat d'or rapportera.

7 Ah, dites-moi, ma mèr' ô grand',
  Qu'ont les valets à soupirer?
  – C'est leurs chevaux qu'ils ont baignés;
  Un beau cheval ils ont noyé.

1 She looked out from the turret high
  And saw her own son riding nigh.
  – My son Renaud, my dearest one,
  Your wife has borne to you a son.

2 – Not for my wife nor for my son
  Can I rejoice; my day is done,
  For I have taken a deep death-stroke.
  I hold my bowels in my cloak.

3 Mother, go in and make my bed,
  And make it neat from foot to head.
  All white and neat my bed must be;
  But my sweet wife must not see me.

4 And when the midnight hour did toll,
  Renaud delivered up his soul.
  The servant-girls so loudly cried;
  Likewise the grooms did mourn and sigh.

5 – My lady mother, tell me why
  Our servant-girls do weep and cry?
  – There in the kitchen as they washed,
  A golden platter they have lost.

6 – For a gold dish that's gone astray
  There is no call to weep and cry.
  When my Renaud comes back from war
  We shall have golden plates in store.

7 – My lady mother, tell me why
  All my young grooms do mourn and
                              sigh?
  – As they were running by yon sea-side,
  One of the mares drowned in the tide.

CANADA

8 – Pour un cheval qu'ils ont noyé,
Ma mère, faut-il tant soupirer?
Quand Renaud de guerre viendra,
Un beau cheval ramènera.

(*spoken*)
Quand le matin fut arrivé,
La bière il a fallu clouer.

(*sung*)
9 – Ah, dites-moi, mère m'ami',
Ce que j'entends cogner ainsi?
– C'est le petit dauphin qu'est né;
La tapisserie leur faut clouer.

10 Le dimanche étant arrivé,
A l'églis' il lui faut aller.
Le rouge elle devait porter
Mais le noir lui fut présenté.

11 – Ah, dites-moi, mère m'ami',
Pourquoi changez-vous mes habits?
– A toute femm' qu'élève enfant
Le noir est toujours plus séant.

12 En passant par le grand chemin
Ont fait rencontre de pèlerins.
– Vrai Dieu, voilà de beaux habits
Pour une femme sans mari!

13 – Ah, dites-moi, mère m'ami',
Ce que les petits passants ont dit?
– Ma fille, les passants ont dit
Que vous aviez de beaux habits.

14 A l'église est arrivé'.
Un cierge lui ont présenté.
– Sont les cloches que j'entends sonner.
Le coup de mort ell's ont donné.

15 Ma mère, voici un tombeau;
Jamais n'en ai vu de si beau.
– Ma fill', ne puis vous le cacher;
Le beau Renaud a trépassé.

16 – Vrai Dieu, puisque c'est mon mari,
Je veux m'en aller avec lui.
Ma mer', retournez au château.
Prenez soin du petit nouveau.

8 – Oh, for a mare drowned in the tide
There is no call to mourn and sigh.
When my Renaud comes back from war
He will bring many a handsome mare.

(*spoken*)
But when the morning dawned so clear.
They drove the nails into the bier.

(*sung*)
9 – Come tell to me, my mother dear,
What is that hammering noise I hear?
– All on account of your young baby,
The men are nailing the tapestry.

10 And so when Sunday came around,
Off to the church they all were bound.
She had a mind to wear the red,
But she was given the black instead.

11 – Come tell to me, my mother dear.
Why have you changed the dress I wear?
– For a young wife with babe at breast
Modest and seemly black is best.

12 As they walked on the broad highway,
A band of pilgrims they passed by.
– Great God, and here's a handsome
                                    gown
For a young wife who's lost her man.

13 – O mother dear, tell me, I pray,
What did those little pilgrims say?
– My dearest daughter, I heard them
                                    swear
By the fine dress that you do wear.

14 And now within the church she stands.
A lighted candle in her hand.
– I hear the passing-bell to toll;
It is the knell of some poor soul.

15 Here is a grave both wide and deep;
The finest grave my eyes did see.
– Daughter, the truth I cannot hide;
This is the grave where Renaud lies.

16 – If here's the grave of my Renaud,
Along with him then I will go.
O mother, homeward you must turn,
And cherish well my little son.

A. L. L.

3

2 ISABEAU S'Y PROMÈNE

Isabeau goes a-walking

I - sa - beau s'y pro - mè - ne
Le long de son jar - din, ___ Le long de
son jar-din Sur le bord de l'î - le, Le long de
son jar-din Sur le bord de l'eau, Sur le bord du vais-seau.

1 Isabeau s'y promène
Le long de son jardin,
Le long de son jardin
  Sur le bord de l'île,
Le long de son jardin
  Sur le bord de l'eau,
  Sur le bord du vaisseau.

2 Elle fit un' rencontre
De trente matelots,
De trente matelots
  Sur le bord de l'île, etc.

3 Le plus jeune des trente,
Il se mit à chanter,
Il se mit à chanter
  Sur le bord de l'île, etc.

4 La chanson que tu chantes,
Je voudrais la savoir,
Je voudrais la savoir
  Sur le bord de l'île, etc.

1 Isabeau goes a-walking
All in her garden fair,
All in her garden fair
  By the little island,
All in her garden fair
  By the waterside,
  By the banks of the sea.

2 And what should she spy there
But thirty seamen bold,
But thirty seamen bold
  By the little island, etc.

3 The youngest of the sailors.
He started in to sing,
He started in to sing
  By the little island, etc.

4 The song that you are singing
Is one I'd like to learn,
Is one I'd like to learn
  By the little island, etc.

5 Embarque dans ma barque,
  Je te la chanterai,
  Je te la chanterai
    Sur le bord de l'île, etc.

6 Quand ell' fut dans la barque,
  Ell' se mit à pleurer,
  Ell' se mit à pleurer
    Sur le bord de l'île, etc.

7 Qu'avez-vous donc, la belle,
  Qu'a-vous à tant pleurer?
  Qu'a vous à tant pleurer
    Sur le bord de l'île, etc.

8 Je pleure mon anneau d'ore,
  Dans l'eau-z-il est tombé,
  Dans l'eau-z-il est tombé
    Sur le bord de l'île, etc.

9 Ne pleurez point, la belle,
  Je vous le plongerai,
  Je vous le plongerai
    Sur le bord de l'île, etc.

10 De la première plonge
   Il n'a rien ramené,
   Il n'a rien ramené
     Sur le bord de l'île, etc.

11 De la seconde plonge
   L'anneau-z-a voltigé,
   L'anneau-z-a voltigé
     Sur le bord de l'île, etc.

12 De la troisième plonge
   Le galant s'est noyé,
   Le galant s'est noyé
     Sur le bord de l'île.
   Le galant s'est noyé
     Sur le bord de l'eau,
     Sur le bord du vaisseau.

5 Well, come aboard, my handsome,
  And I'll teach you my song,
  And I'll teach you my song
    By the little island, etc.

6 Well, once aboard the frigate,
  So bitterly she wept,
  So bitterly she wept
    By the little island, etc.

7 What ails you now, my sweetheart,
  That makes you weep and mourn?
  That makes you weep and mourn
    By the little island, etc.

8 I'm weeping for my gold ring
  That's fallen in the sea,
  That's fallen in the sea
    By the little island, etc.

9 Oh, dry your eyes, my darling,
  I'll dive and bring it back,
  I'll dive and bring it back
    By the little island, etc.

10 The first time that he dived in,
   Oh, nothing could he find,
   Oh, nothing could he find
     By the little island, etc.

11 The second time he dived in,
   The ring began to roll,
   The ring began to roll
     By the little island, etc.

12 The third time that he dived in
   Her sailor boy was drowned,
   Her sailor boy was drowned
     By the little island,
   Her sailor boy was drowned
     By the waterside
     By the banks of the sea.
                                A. L. L.

CANADA

3 BLANCHE COMME LA NEIGE

White as Snow

La bell' s'est en-dor-mi'_____ sur un beau iit de
ro - ses, La ro - ses, Blan - che com-me la
nei - ge, bell' com-me le jour; Ils_ sont trois
ca - pi - tai - nes qui vont lui fair' l'a - mour.

1 La bell' s'est endormi' sur un beau lit de roses, (2)
   Blanche comme la neige, bell' comme le jour;
   Ils sont trois capitaines qui vont lui fair' l'amour.

2 Le plus jeune des trois la prend par sa main blanche : (2)
   Montez, montez, princesse, dessus mon cheval gris;
   À Paris je vous mène dans un fort beau logis.

3 Tout aussitôt rendus, l'hôtesse lui demande : (2)
   Àh, dites-moi, la belle, dites-moi sans mentir,
   Êt'-vous ici par force ou pour vos bons plaisirs?

4 La bell' a repondu : Je suis un' fille sage. (2)
   Au château de mon père les gens du roi m'ont pris,
   M'ont pris, m'ont emmenée a ce fort beau logis.

5 Finissant ce discours, le capitaine rentre : (2)
   Mangez, buvez, la belle, selon votre appétit;
   Avec un capitaine vous passerez la nuit.

6 Au milieu du repas, la belle a tombé morte. (2)
   Sonnez, sonnez les cloches, tambours au régiment!
   Ma maîtress', elle est morte à l'âge de quinz' ans!

7 Où l'enterrerons-nous, cett' aimable princesse? (2)
Au jardin de son père, dessous un pommier gris.
Nous prierons Dieu pour elle qu'elle aill' en paradis.

8 Mais au bout de trois jour son père s'y promène. (2)
Ouvrez, ouvrez ma tombe, mon pèr', si vous m'aimez!
Trois jours j'ai fait la morte pour mon honneur garder.

1 A fair maid lay asleep upon a bed of roses, (2)
White as snow freshly fallen and fair as morning sky;
Three fine and noble captains on her they cast an eye.

2 The youngest of the three her milk-white hand has taken. (2)
Mount, O mount, lovely princess, upon my grey-white steed;
To lodgings fine in Paris I'll take you with all speed.

3 No sooner was she there, the hostess asked her kindly: (2)
Tell me why you have come here and tell the truth I pray;
Were you a-seeking pleasure or were you stol'n away?

4 I am a virtuous maid, and this I tell you truly, (2)
From my own father's castle the soldiers of the king
Have stolen me and brought me unto this fine lodging.

5 These words no sooner said when back returned the captain (2)
Eat and drink, lovely fair one, and ease your appetite.
For with a noble captain you'll pass this livelong night.

6 She'd taken but one bite when down she fell a-dying. (2)
Beat the drum, toll the church bells, let all the comp'ny weep,
For I have lost my sweetheart, her age was scarce fifteen.

7 Where shall we dig her grave? O where shall she be buried? (2)
In her own father's garden beneath the apple tree.
We pray that soon this damsel in paradise may be.

8 And when three days had passed her father went a-walking. (2)
Open quick, dearest father, release me from the grave.
Three days and nights I've lain here my honour for to save.

M. K.

4 QUAND J'ÉTAIS CHEZ MON PÈRE

When I was with my father

Quand j'é-tais chez mon pè - re, Quand j'é-tais chez mon pè - re, Pe-tit' et jeun' é - tions, Don-dai-ne don, Pe - tit' et jeun' é - tions, Don - dai - ne.

1 Quand j'étais chez mon père (2)
  Petit' et jeun' étions,
    Dondaine don,
  Petit' et jeun' étions,
    Dondaine.

2 M'envoi'-t-a la fontain' (2)
  Pour pêcher du poisson.

3 La fontain' est profonde (2)
  J'me suis coulé' au fond.

4 Par ici-t-il y passe (2)
  Trois cavaliers barons.

5 Que donn'riez-vous, belle (2)
  Qui vous tir'rait du font?

6 Tirez, tirez, dit-elle, (2)
  Apres ça, nous verrons.

1 When I was with my father, (2)
  Pretty and young was I,
    Down derry die
  Pretty and young was I.
    Down derry.

2 They sent me to the fountain (2)
  Fishes to catch I tried.

3 I fell into the fountain, (2)
  There I was forced to lie.

4 Just at that very moment (2)
  Three cavaliers passed by.

5 If from the pond we pull you (2)
  What shall we have as prize?

6 First pull me from the fountain (2)
  Then we will see, said I.

7 Quand la bell' fut tirée, (2)
S'en fut à la maison.

7 When from the pond they'd pulled her.
(2)
They to her home did ride.

8 S'assit sur la fenêtre, (2)
Compose une chanson.

8 She from an open window (2)
Sang them a fond good-bye.

9 Ce n'est pas ça, la belle, (2)
Que nous vous demandons.

9 We do not want your singing, (2)
That is too poor a prize.

10 C'est votre coeur en gage, (2)
Savoir si nous l'aurons.

10 We want to have your kisses, (2)
To be your heart's delight.

11 Mon petit coeur en gage (2)
N'est pas pour un baron.

11 No cavalier shall kiss me, (2)
Nor be my heart's delight.

12 Ma mère me le garde (2)
Pour mon joli mignon,
Dondaine don,
Pour mon joli mignon,
Dondaine.

12 I have my own true lover; (2)
He is my heart's delight.
Down derry die
He is my heart's delight.
Down derry.

M. K.

5 LA SAINTE VIERGE AUX CHEVEUX PENDANTS

The Blessed Virgin of Unbraided Hair

La sain-te Vierg' s'en va chan - tant, A - vec ses longs che - veux pen - dants. Dans son che - min a ren - con - tré Un bou-lan-ger, un bou-lan - ger. Bon bou-lan-ger, bon bou-lan - ger, Veux - tu don- ner un pain pour Dieu? Le bou-lan - ger, pris de pi - tié, Trois pe-tits pains lui a don - nés.

1 La sainte Vierg' s'en va chantant,
Avec ses longs cheveux pendants.
Dans son chemin a rencontré
Un boulanger, un boulanger.
Bon boulanger, bon boulanger,
Veux-tu donner un pain pour Dieu?
Le boulanger, pris de pitié,
Trois petits pains lui a donnés.

1 Our Blessed Virgin sang so clear.
Her hair unbraided she did wear.
She met a baker on her way,
And to this baker she did say:
Good baker, of your charity,
Pray give a loaf of bread to me.
His heart was filled with great pity;
Three loaves he gave to Our Lady.

2 La sainte Vierg' s'en va chantant,
Avec ses longs cheveux pendants.
Dans sen chemin a rencontré
Un charbonnier; a demandé:
Bon charbonnier, bon charbonnier,
Veux-tu donner du feu pour Dieu?
Le charbonnier, point de pitié,
Trois coups de pied lui a donnés.

3 La sainte Vierg' s'en va pleurant,
Avec ses longs cheveux pendants.
Dans son chemin a rencontré
Un' jeune fill', a demandé:
Bell' jeune fill', bell' jeune fill'
Veux-tu donner ton sang pour Dieu?
La jeune fill', pris' de pitié,
Trois goutt's de sang lui a donnés.

4 La sainte Vierg' s'en va chantant,
Avec ses longs cheveux pendants.
Le boulanger, il fut sauvé;
Le charbonnier, il fut damné.
La jeune fille avec Marie
S'en est allée au paradis.
La sainte Vierg' s'en va chantant,
Avec ses longs cheveux pendants.

2 Our Blessed Virgin sang so clear.
Her hair unbraided she did wear.
Presently meeting on her way
A charcoal-burner, she did say:
I beg you of your charity,
Pray give a little warmth to me.
Cold was his heart without pity;
Three kicks he gave to Our Lady.

3 Our Blessed Virgin shed a tear.
Her hair unbraided she did wear.
She met a maiden on her way;
Thus to the maiden she did say:
Fair maiden, of your charity,
One drop of blood, pray give to me.
Her heart was filled with great pity;
Three drops she gave to Our Lady.

4 Our Blessed Virgin sang so clear.
Her hair unbraided she did wear.
Saved was the baker, all was well:
The charcoal-burner's damned in hell;
To Paradise the maid has gone,
To be with Mary and her Son.
Our Blessed Virgin sang so clear.
Her hair unbraided she did wear.

M. K.

6 LE LONG DE LA MER JOLIE

All on the blue sea a-sailing

1 Bell', em-bar-quez, bell', em-bar-quez, Dans mon gen-til na-vi-re, Le long de la mer,___ la jo-li' mer,___ Le long de la mer jo-li-e.___ 2 Mais quand la bell' fut em-bar-qué', Ell' rou-git, ell' sou-pi-re. Qu'a-vez-vous, qu'a-vez-vous donc, Qu'a-vous à sou-pi-rer?_ Le long de la mer,___ La jo-li' mer,_ Le long de la mer jo-li-e.___

1 Bell', embarquez, bell', embarquez
Dans mon gentil navire,
   Le long de la mer, la joli' mer,
   Le long de la mer jolie.

1 Come pretty maid, aboard my ship
To sail over the ocean.
   A-sailing the sea, the deep blue sea,
   All on the blue sea a-sailing.

2 Mais quand la bell' fut embarqué',
Ell' rougit, ell' soupire.
Qu'avez-vous, qu'avez-vous donc,
   Qu'a'-vous à soupirer?

2 She came aboard to join the sailor
And sat, weeping and sighing.
What is the matter, my fair maid?
O why are you a-crying?

3 Mon beau galant, si tu savais
De qui je suis la fille!
Je suis la fille du bourreau,
Le plus gros de la ville.

3 I fear my father, sir, she said,
He'll ne'er show any pity.
He is a hangman cruel, she said,
The worst man in the city.

CANADA

4 Bell', débarquez, bell' débarquez
  De mon gentil navire!
  Quand la bell' fut débarqué,
  Ell' ne faisait que rire.

5 Le marinier a demandé:
  Qu'avez-vous, bell' à tant rire?
  Mon beau galant, si tu savais
  De qui je suis la fille!

6 Je suis la fille du bourgeois,
  Le plus rich' de la ville.
  Bell' revenez, bell' revenez!
  Je vous donn'rai cent livres!

7 Ni pour un cent, ni pour deux cents,
  Ni pour cent mille livres.
  Il faut plumer la perdrix
  Tandis qu'elle est prise.
    Le long de la mer, la joli' mer,
    Le long de la mer jolie.

4 Then disembark, my fair young maid,
  'Tis time that we were parted.
  She disembarked and, standing on shore,
  She laughed, gay and light-hearted.

5 Pray tell to me, my fair young maid,
  The cause of all this laughter.
  I have not told you truly, she said,
  Of whom I am the daughter.

6 My father has great houses and land,
  The best man in the city.
  Come back on board and you shall have
  In gold one hundred guineas.

7 Not for a hundred pounds, she said,
  Will I come back on board, sir.
  You should have plucked the partridge
                  wild
  As soon as you had caught her.
    A-sailing the sea, the deep blue sea,
    All on the blue sea a-sailing.

                            M. K.

7 DANS LES HAUBANS

In the Rigging

J'ai fait fair' un beau na - vi - re, un na - vir', un bâ - ti - ment. L'é - qui - pag' qui le gou - ver - ne sont des fil - les de quinz' ans. Sau - tons, lé - gè-res ber - gè - res, dan-sons là lé - gè - re - ment!

1 J'ai fait fair' un beau navire, un navir', un bâtiment.
   L'équipag' qui le gouverne sont des filles de quinz' ans.
   Sautons, légères bergères, dansons là légèrement!

2 L'equipag' qui le gouverne sont des filles de quinze ans.
   Moi qui suis garçon bon drille, j'me suis engagé dedans.

3 Moi qui suis garçon bon drille, j'me suis engagé dedans.
   J'ai aperçu ma maitresse qui dormait dans les haubans.

4 J'ai aperçu ma maitresse qui dormait dans les haubans.
   J'ai r'connu son blanc corsage, son visage souriant.

5 J'ai r'connu son blanc corsage, son visage souriant.
   J'ai aperçu ses mains fines, ses cheveux dans un ruban.

6 J'ai aperçu ses mains fines, ses cheveux dans un ruban.
   Suis monté dans les cordages, aupres d'elle dans les haubans.

7 Suis monté dans les cordages, aupres d'elle dans les haubans.
   Lui ai parlé d'amourette. Elle m'a dit: Sois mon amant!
   Sautons, légères bergères, dansons là légèrement!

CANADA

1 I have built a handsome ship, a shining ship all on the sea,
   And the crew that works my ship, oh, they're all maids of sweet sixteen.
     Up then, my lively lasses, skip and go so merrily!

2 And the crew that works my ship, oh, they're all maids of sweet sixteen.
   I'm a brisk and airy lad, and such a crew I've never seen.

3 I'm a brisk and airy sailor, never sailed with such a crowd.
   From the deck I spied my sweetheart, lain aloft among the shrouds.

4 From the deck I spied my sweetheart, fast asleep among the sails,
   And I knew her by her bodice, likewise by her lovely smile.

5 And I knew her by her bodice, by her face so sweet and fair,
   Likewise by her slender fingers and the ribbon in her hair.

6 Dainty hands and snow-white bodice, and her hair in ribbons tied.
   In a trice I climbed the rigging till I swung there by her side.

7 In a trice I climbed the rigging till I swung there by her side.
   There I told her of my fancy. 'Be my love!' this young girl cried.
     Up then, my lively lasses, skip and go so merrily!

                                                              A. L. L.

15

8 J'AI CUEILLI LA BELLE ROSE

I have picked the loveliest rose

J'ai cueil-li la bel-le ro-se qui pen-dait au ro-sier blanc. blanc. Je l'ai cueil-li___ feuill' à feuill'. Mon tab-li-er l'ai mis de - dans. Ey-um ta-dl-um, ta-dl-a, i-ya-dl-um, Ey-a ta-dl-a, ta-dl-um, i-ye-dl-a.

1 J'ai cueilli la belle rose qui pendait au rosier blanc. (2)
 Je l'ai cueilli feuill' à feuill'. Mon tablier l'ai mis dedans.
   Eyum ta-dl-um, ta-dl-la, i-ya-dl-um,
   Eya ta-dl-la, ta-dl-lum, i-ye-dl-la.

2 Je l'ai porté à mon père, entre Paris et Rouen. (2)
 Mais je n'y ai vu personne que le rossignol chantant.

3 Il disait dans son langage: Marie-toi, il en est temps! (2)
 Comment veux-tu que j'm'y marie? Mon pèr' il n'y est pas consent.

4 Ni mon père, ni ma mère, ni aucun de mes parents. (2)
 J'm'en irai en service, en service pour un an.

5 Combien gagnez-vous, la belle, combien gagnez-vous par an? (2)
 Je gagnerai cinq cents livres, ou, plus encore, six cents!

6 Venez avec moi, la belle, je vous en donnerai autant,
 Et vous n'aurez rien à faire que mon petit lit de camp.
 À le fair' et le defaire; vous et moi couch'rons dedans.
   Eyum ta-dl-lum, ta-dl-la, i-ya-dl-um,
   Eya ta-dl-la, ta-dl-lum, i-ye-dl-la.

CANADA

1 I have picked the loveliest rose that e'er the sun did shine upon; (2)
I picked its leaves one by one and wrapped them in my aperon.
    Eyum ta-dl-lum, ta-dl-la, i-ya-dl-um,
    Eya ta-dl-la, ta-dl-lum, i-ye-dl-la.

2 To my father's house I came between fair Paris and Rouen (2)
No-one was there, but I heard a nightingale who sang this song:

3 You should marry, pretty maid; 'tis time that you a bride should be. (2)
How can that be, when I know my father he would ne'er agree.

4 And my mother would refuse and all my kin would say me Nay. (2)
So into service I'll go and for a year or more I'll stay.

5 How much money would you earn? O pretty maid, I pray come tell; (2)
Five hundred pounds I would earn and may be seven pence as well.

6 Come with me, my pretty maid, and you shall earn as much or more.
And your only work will be to make my little bed of straw;
And when 'tis made, you and I we'll lie in it for evermore.
    Eyum ta-dl-lum, ta-dl-la, i-ya-dl-um,
    Eya ta-dl-la, ta-dl-lum, i-te-dl-la.

M. K.

9 LÀ-HAUT SUR CES MONTAGNES

High on the top of a mountain

Là-haut sur ces mon - ta - gnes, —
J'ai en-ten-du pleu - rer. Oh! — c'est la —
voix — de ma maî - tres - se; — Il — faut al -
ler la — con - so - ler. — C'est la voix de ma maî -
tres - se; Il — faut al - ler la — con - so - ler.

1 Là-haut sur ces montagnes,
J'ai entendu pleurer.
Oh! c'est la voix de ma maîtresse; ⎫
Il faut aller la consoler. ⎭ (2)

2 Qu'avez-vous donc, bergère,
Qu'avez-vous à tant pleurer?
Ah, si je pleur' c'est de tendresse; ⎫
C'est de vous avoir trop aimé. ⎭ (2)

1 High on the top of a mountain
I heard a maiden cry.
O 'tis the voice of my sweetheart; ⎫
For to console her I'll draw nigh. ⎭ (2)

2 Shepherdess, tell me what ails you?
Why do you weep and sigh?
You are the cause of my weeping; ⎫
For love of you I fain would die. ⎭ (2)

3 De tant s'aimer, la belle,
  Qui nous empêchera?
  Faudrait avoir un coeur de pierre } (2)
  À qui ne vous aimerait pas.

4 Les moutons dans ces plaines
  Sont en danger des loups.
  Pas plus que vous, belle bergère, } (2)
  Vous qui êt's en danger d'amour.

5 Les agneaux vive' a l'herbe,
  Les papillons aux fleurs.
  Et toi et moi, jolie bergère,
  Pourquoi n'y vivre qu'en langueur? } (2)

3 And who's to stop us from loving?
  Love cannot be denied.
  I'd have a heart made of granite } (2)
  Did I not seek you for my bride.

4 Look at my sheep, they're in danger.
  Wolves are upon the hill.
  You are in just as great danger; } (2)
  Love is a weapon that can kill.

5 Butterflies feed on the flowers;
  Sheep on the grass so green.
  Why should not I and my sweetheart } (2)
  Live without care in love serene.

M. K.

10 EN ROULANT MA BOULE

Roll, my ball, a-rolling

Der - rièr' chez nous y'a - t-un é - tang, En rou-lant ma
bou - le, Trois beaux ca-nards s'en vont bai-gnant, Rouli, rou-lant, ma bou-le-ti rou - lant, Rou-lant ma
bou - le - ti roul', En rou-lant ma bou - le.

1 Derrièr' chez nous y'a-t-un étang,
   En roulant ma boule,
Trois beaux canards s'en vont baignant,
   Rouli, roulant, ma boule-ti roulant,
   Roulant ma boule-ti roul',
   En roulant ma boule.

2 Trois beaux canards s'en vont baignant.
   Le fils du roi s'en va chassant.

3 Le fils du roi s'en va chassant
   Avec son grand fusil d'argent.

1 Behind our house there is a pond,
   Roll, my ball, a-rolling,
Three pretty ducks go swimming round.
   So roll around, my rollicky roley,
   Roll on, my rollicky roll,
   Roll, my ball, a-rolling.

2 A-hunting goes the king's own son,
   Roll, my ball, a-rolling,
All with his shining silver gun,
   So roll along, my rollicky roley,
   Roll on, my rollicky roll,
   Roll, my ball, a-rolling.

3 With his long gun that shines so bright.
   Roll, my ball, a-rolling,
Aims at the black and shoots the white.
   So roll aright, my rollicky roley,
   Roll on, my rollicky roll,
   Roll, my ball, a-rolling.

CANADA

4 Avec son grand fusil d'argent,
   Visa le noir, tua le blanc.

5 Visa le noir, tua le blanc.
   O fils du roi, tu es méchant.

6 O fils du roi, tu es méchant,
   D'avoir tué mon canard blanc.

7 D'avoir tué mon canard blanc.
   Par les yeux lui sort'nt des diamants.

8 Par les yeux lui sort'nt des diamants,
   Et par le bec, l'or et l'argent.

9 Et par le bec, l'or et l'argent.
   Toutes ses plum's s'en vont aux vents.

10 Toutes ses plum's s'en vont aux vents.
   Trois dam's s'en vont les ramassant.

11 Trois dam's s'en vont les ramassant,
   C'est pour en fair' un lit de camp.

12 C'est pour en fair' un lit de camp,
   En roulant ma boule.
   Pour y coucher tous les passants,
     Rouli, roulant, ma boule-ti roulant,
     Roulant ma boule-ti roul',
     En roulant ma boule.

4 O prince, now may you have bad luck.
   Roll, my ball, a-rolling,
   For you have shot my handsome duck.
     So roll 'em up, my rollicky roley.
     Roll on, my rollicky roll,
     Roll, my ball, a-rolling.

5 Diamonds from his eyes do spill,
   Roll, my ball, a-rolling,
   And gold and silver from his bill,
     So roll uphill, my rollicky roley.
     Roll on, my rollicky roll,
     Roll, my ball, a-rolling.

6 His feathers fly off in the wind,
   Roll, my ball, a-rolling.
   Three ladies go a-gathering them,
     So roll again, my rollicky roley.
     Roll on, my rollicky roll,
     Roll, my ball, a-rolling.

7 To make a mattress on the ground,
   Roll, my ball, a-rolling,
   Where passers-by may rest so sound.
     So roll around, my rollicky roley.
     Roll on, my rollicky roll,
     Roll, my ball, a-rolling.
                              A. L. L.

11 LISETTE

Li - set - te, fais - moi un_ bou - quet,_____ qu'il

soit bien_____ fait! Qu'il soit de roses et de_feuil - les_

ver - tes, c'est ma cou - leur! Je t'ai - me - rai, chè - re Li -

set - te, de tout_ mon_____ coeur.

1 Lisette, fais-moi un bouquet, qu'il soit bien fait!
  Qu'il soit de roses et de feuilles vertes, c'est ma couleur!
  Je t'aimerai, chère Lisette, de tout mon coeur.

2 Lisett', en faisant ce bouquet, elle pleurait.
  Ah! Qu'avez-vous, chère Lisette, a tant pleurer?
  Je suis venu ici, la belle, vous consoler.

3 J'ai bien le sujet de pleurer, vous me quittez.
  Vous allez partir pour les îles: vous m'oublierez.
  En attendant de vos nouvelles, je languirai.

4 Lisett', si tu voulais m'aimer, je reviendrais.
  Appell' ton per', aussi ta mere: et moi, les miens.
  Unissons nos deux coeurs ensemble, je le veux bien!

CANADA

1 Lisette, come make me a bouquet both fine and gay.
Take a red rose and some green leaves; I tell you true
That I will love you, dear Lisette, the whole year through.

2 Lisette, as she made this bouquet, began to cry
What ails you now, my sweet Lisette, why do you weep?
For I'm come here, my pretty one, to give you ease.

3 Well may I weep: I heard them say you're leaving me.
You're sailing to some foreign land, where you'll forget,
While I do wait for news of you with heavy heart.

4 Lisette, if you will love me true, I will return.
Go call your parents from the house and I'll call mine.
We'll join our hands in wedded bands ere summertime.

A. L. L.

12 DANS LES CHANTIERS NOUS HIVERNERONS

A-wintering up in the lumber-camp

Voi - ci l'hi - ver ar - ri - vé, Les ri - viè - res
sont ge - lées; C'est le temps d'al - ler au bois,
Man - ger_ du lard et des pois. Dans les chan - tiers nous hi -
ver - ne - rons! Dans les chan - tiers nous hi - ver - ne - rons.

1 Voici l'hiver arrivé,
　Les rivières sont gelées;
　C'est le temps d'aller au bois,
　Manger du lard et des pois.
　　Dans les chantiers nous hivernerons!
　　Dans les chantiers nous hivernerons!

1 Now the winter's come at last,
　And the river's frozen fast,
　Off we go among the trees,
　Live on lard and black-eyed peas.
　　A-wintering up in the lumber-camp!
　　A-wintering up in the lumber-camp!

2 Pauv' voyageur, que t'as d'la misere!
　Souvent tu couches par terre;
　A la pluie, au mauvais temps,
　A la rigueur de tous les temps!

2 Hard, hard times, boys, all around!
　Sometimes sleeping on the ground;
　Rain or hailstorm, frost or snow,
　With our axes out we go!

3 Quand tu arriv' a Quebec,
　Souvent tu fais un gros bec.
　Tu vas trouver ton bourgeois
　Qu'est là assis a son comptoi'.

3 When you get up to Quebec,
　Like as not you'll feel a wreck.
　To the boss you make your way,
　Hoping for to draw your pay.

CANADA

4 Je voudrais être payé
   Pour le temps que j'ai donné.
   Quand l'bourgeois est en banqu'route,
   Il te renvoi' manger des croûtes.

5 Quand tu retourn' chez ton père,
   Aussi pour revoir ta mère;
   Le bonhomme est à la porte,
   La bonn'femme fait la gargotte.

6 Ah! bonjour donc, mon cher enfant!
   Nous apport'-tu ben d'l'argent?
   Que l'diable emport' les chantiers!
   Jamais d'ma vie j'y r'tournerai!
     Dans les chantiers, ah! n'hivernons
                                  plus!
     Dans les chantiers, ah! n'hivernons
                                  plus!

4 Pay me down my money now
   For the time I worked for you!
   If by chance the boss is broke,
   All your dreams go up in smoke.

5 When you get home with your pay,
   They'll all greet their shanty-boy.
   Father standing at the gate,
   Mother with the old soup-plate.

6 It's: Good day, my dearest son!
   How much money have you brought
                                  home?
   Devil take that old pine shack!
   Never again will I go back!
     A-wintering up in the lumber-camp!
     A-wintering up in the lumber-camp!
                                  A. L. L.

25

13 THE BONNY BANKS OF THE VIRGIE O

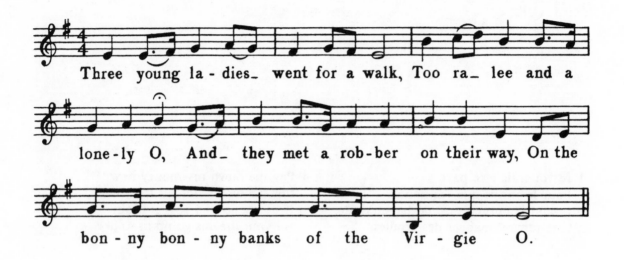

1. Three young ladies went for a walk,
    Too ra lee and a lonely O,
   And they met a robber on their way,
    On the bonny bonny banks of the
      Virgie O.

2. He took the first one by the hand.
   He whipped her round till he made her
      stand.

3. Oh, will you be a robber's wife,
   Or will you die by my penknife?

4. I will not be a robber's wife;
   I'd rather die by your penknife.

5. Oh, he took out his little penknife,
   And it's then he took her own sweet life.

6. He took the second one by the hand.
   He whipped her round till he made her
      stand.

7. Oh, will you be a robber's wife,
   Or will you die by my penknife?

8. I will not be a robber's wife;
   I'd rather die by your penknife.

9. Oh, he took out his little penknife,
   And it's then he took her own sweet life.

10. He took the third one by the hand.
    He whipped her round till he made her
       stand.

11. Oh, will you be a robber's wife,
    Or will you die by my penknife?

12. I will not be a robber's wife,
    Nor will I die by your penknife.

13. Oh, if my brothers had been here
    You'd not have killed my sisters dear.

14. What is your brothers, come tell to me?
    The one is a minister, sir, said she.

15. What did the other, I pray you tell?
    Oh, he is a robber like yoursel'.

16. Lord have mercy for what I've done:
    I've murdered my three sisters all but
       one!

17. Oh, he took out his little penknife,
    Too ra lee and a lonely O,
    And it's then he took his own sweet life.
    On the bonny bonny banks of the
       Virgie O.

14 THE LOVER'S GHOST

John - ny he pro - mis'd to mar - ry me, But I
fear he's with some fair one_ gone. There's_
some-thing be-wails him and I don't know what it is, And_ I'm
wea - ry from ly - ing a - lone.___

1 Johnny he promis'd to marry me,
But I fear he's with some fair one gone.
There's something bewails him and I don't know what it is.
And I'm weary from lying alone.

2 John he came there at the hour appointed;
He tapped at the window so low.
This fair maid arose and she hurried on her clothes,
And welcomed her true love home.

3 She took him by the hand and laid him down;
She felt he was colder than clay.
She said: My dearest dear, if I only had my wish
This long night would never be day.

4 Crow up, crow up, my little bird,
And don't you crow before day,
And your cage shall be made of the glittering gold, she says,
And your doors of the silver so gay.

5 Where is your soft bed of down, my love,
And where is your white holland sheet,
And where is the fair maid that watches on you
While you are taking your long silent sleep?

6 The sand is my soft bed of down, my love,
The sea is my white holland sheet,
And long hungry worms will feed off of me
While I sleep every night in the deep.

7 O when will I see you, my love, she cries,
And when will I see you again?
When the little fishes fly and the seas they do run dry
And the hard rocks they melt with the sun.

15 OH, WHO IS AT MY BEDROOM WINDOW?

Oh, who is at my bed-room win-dow, Dis-tur-bing me from my night's rest? It is, it is your own true lov-er, The ve-ry one that_ you love best.

1 Oh, who is at my bedroom window,
Disturbing me from my night's rest?
It is, it is your own true lover,
The very one that you love best.

2 Go, Maggie dear, go ask your father,
See if our wedding bride may be.
If he says 'No', love, come and tell me,
And I'll no longer troubled be.

3 It is no use of asking father,
For he is on his bed of rest,
And by his side a silver dagger
To stab the one that he loves best.

4 Go, Maggie dear, go ask your mother,
See if our wedding bride may be.
If she says 'No', love, come and tell me,
And I'll no longer troubled be.

5 It is no use of asking mother,
For she is on to set us free.
You'd better go and court some other,
For you cannot marry me.

6 I can climb the highest mountains,
I can rob the eagle's nest,
I can court some other,
But you're the one that I love best.

7 She drew the dagger from her pocket
And buried it deep, deep in her breast,
Sang adieu to her cruel parents:
I'll die with the one that I love best.

8 He drew the dagger from her bosom
And buried it deep, deep in his breast,
Sang adieu to her cruel parents,
And she died with the one that she loved
best.

16 THE GYPSY LADDIE

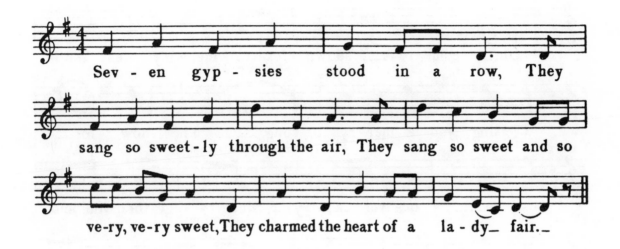

Sev- en gyp - sies stood in a row, They sang so sweet-ly through the air, They sang so sweet and so ve-ry, ve-ry sweet, They charmed the heart of a la - dy_ fair._

1 Seven gypsies stood in a row,
They sang so sweetly through the air,
They sang so sweet and so very, very
sweet,
They charmed the heart of a lady fair.

2 She was sitting in her castle high,
Smiling on those gypsies O;
Some jealous thought came into her mind,
She would follow the dark-eyed gypsies O.

3 When the lord came home that night,
Enquiring for his lady O,
I'm afraid, I'm afraid, says the old
kitchen maid,
That she followed the dark-eyed gypsies
O.

4 Saddle my horse, come saddle my team,
And brace my pistols by my side
That I may ride till broad daylight
And follow the dark-eyed gypsy O.

5 He rode West and then rode North
Till he came to a farmer's door.
O farmer, farmer, tell me the truth,
Have you seen the dark-eyed gypsies O?

6 You ride on, the old farmer cried,
Down in yonder valley O,
And there you'll find your own true love
In the arms of a dark-eyed gypsy O.

7 Last night you lay on your feather bed
With blankets round you white as snow,
And tonight you lie on the cold damp
ground
In the arms of a dark-eyed gypsy O.

8 Will you come home, my fair lady,
Will you come home, my honey O,
Or will you forsake your own native
land
And follow the dark-eyed gypsy O?

9 I'll forsake my castle, she said,
And I'll forsake my native land.
I'll eat of the grass and drink of the dew
And follow the dark-eyed gypsy O.

17 THE FALSE YOUNG MAN

1 Oh, come, sit down close to me, my dear,
   While I sing you a merry song.
   'Tis now for us well over a year,
   Since together you and I have been;
   Since together you and I have been, my dear,
   Since together you and I have been.
   'Tis now for us well over a year,
   Since together you and I have been.

CANADA

2　I will not sit close to you, my dear,
　　Not now nor any other time.
　　You've given your love to another one,
　　And your heart no longer is mine.
　　Your heart no longer is mine, my dear,
　　Your heart no longer is mine.
　　You've given your love to another one,
　　And your heart no longer is mine.

3　When your heart truly was mine, my dear,
　　You laid your head upon my breast,
　　And I listened to the strange oaths you swore
　　That the sun it rose in the west;
　　That the sun it rose in the west, my dear,
　　That the sun it rose in the west;
　　And I listened to the strange oaths you swore
　　That the sun it rose in the west.

4　There's a rose in the garden for you, my dear,
　　A rose in the garden for you.
　　When fish fly high like the birds in the sky,
　　Young men will then prove true.
　　Young men will then prove true, my dear,
　　Young men will then prove true.
　　When fish fly high like birds in the sky,
　　Young men will then prove true.

18 THE MAID ON THE SHORE

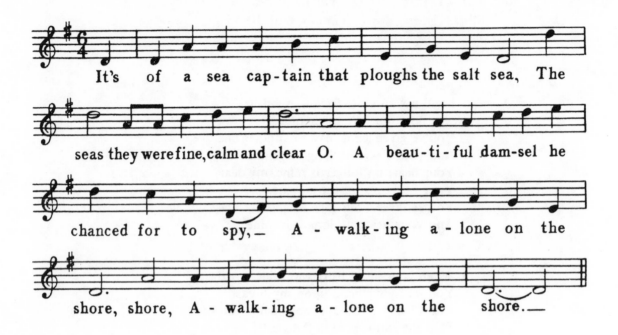

It's of a sea cap-tain that ploughs the salt sea, The seas they were fine, calm and clear O. A beau-ti-ful dam-sel he chanced for to spy,— A-walk-ing a-lone on the shore, shore, A-walk-ing a-lone on the shore.—

1 It's of a sea captain that ploughs the salt sea,
  The seas they were fine, calm and clear O.
  A beautiful damsel he chanced for to spy,
  A-walking alone on the shore, shore,
  A-walking alone on the shore.

2 O what will I give to my sailors so bold?
  Ten guineas I vow and declare O,
  If you'll fetch me that lady on board of my ship
  That walks all alone on the shore, shore,
  That walks all alone on the shore.

3 The sailors did hoist out a very long boat
  And straight for the shore they did steer O,
  Saying: Ma'am, if you please, will you enter on board.
  And view a fine cargo of ware, ware,
  And view a fine cargo of ware.

4 With long persuading they got her on board,
The seas they were fine, calm and clear O.
She sat herself down in the stern of the boat
And straight for the ship they did steer, steer,
And straight from the ship they did steer.

5 And when they arrived alongside of the ship
The captain he ordered a chair O,
Saying: First you shall lie in my arms all this night
And the next you shall marry me, dear, dear,
And the next you shall marry me, dear.

6 She set herself down in the stern of the ship
The seas they were fine, calm and clear O.
She sang so neat, so sweet and complete,
She sang sailors and captain to sleep, sleep,
She sang sailors and captain to sleep.

7 She robbed them of silver, she robbed them of gold,
She robbed them of costly ware O.
The captain's broadsword she took for an oar,
And she paddled away for the shore, shore,
And she paddled away for the shore.

8 When the captain awoke and he found she was gone
He was like a man in despair O.
He called up his men and commanded a boat
To row him away for the shore, shore,
To row him away for the shore.

9 He lowered himself down in the stern of the boat,
And away for the shore they did steer O.
She saluted the captain as well as the crew,
Saying: I'm a maiden once more on the shore, shore,
I'm a maiden once more on the shore.

19 THE MAIDEN'S LAMENT

1 As I roved out one evening in Spring
Down by a silent sweet shady grove,
I heard a maiden making sad lament,
She cried: Alas, I have lost my love.

2 O love is like an unquenching fire,
  Like a raging fire it seems to burn.
  Unto my cold grave I will retire,
  Unto my friends I will ne'er return.

3 Come all you fair maids like me a-dying.
  It's now I'm taking my last farewell.
  And all you small birds round me flying.
  Let your sweet notes be my passing bell.

20 BOLD WOLFE

Come all you young men all, let this de-light you.. Cheer up, you young men all, let no-thing fright you. Ne-ver let your cou-rage fail when you're brought to tri-al, Nor let your fan-cy move at the first de-ni-al.

1 Come all you young men all, let this delight you.
  Cheer up, you young men all, let nothing fright you.
  Never let your courage fail when you're brought to trial.
  Nor let your fancy move at the first denial.

2 I went to see my love, thinking to woo her.
  I sot down by her side, not to undo her;
  But whenever I looks on her, my tongue do quiver;
  I durst not speak one word while I am with her.

3 Love, here's a diamond ring, long years I've kept it.
  Love, here's a chain of gold, if you'll accept it.
  When you view the roses red, think on the giver;
  Madame, remember me, undone forever.

CANADA

4 This brave undaunted youth have crossed the ocean.
To free America was his intention.
He landed at Quebec with all his party,
The city to attack, being brave and hearty.

5 Bold Wolfe drew up his men in a line so pretty;
On the plains of Abraham, before the city.
The French came marching down in hopes to meet them
With a double number round, resolved to beat him.

6 Montcalm and this brave youth together walked,
Between two armies, they like brothers talked.
Till each one to his post then did retire.
'Twas then those numerous hosts began to fire.

7 The drums did loudly beat, the colours flying,
And purple gore did stream and men lay dying;
And shot from off his horse fell that brave hero.
We'll long lament his loss in tears of sorrow.

8 He lifted up his head when guns did rattle,
And to his army said: How goes the battle?
Quebec is all our own, none can prevent it.
Oh then, replies bold Wolfe, I die contented.

21 THE STORMY SCENES OF WINTER

The stor - my scenes of win - ter___ in -
And dark shades o - ver the cen - tres where the

cline_ to frost and snow,___
stor - my winds do blow._ You are the girl I've

cho - sen for to be my on - ly dear;___ Your

scorn-ful heart is fro - zen_ or else_locked up,_ I fear._

1 The stormy scenes of winter incline to frost and snow,
And dark shades over the centres where the stormy winds do blow.
You are the girl I've chosen for to be my only dear;
Your scornful heart is frozen or else locked up, I fear.

2 One night I went to see my love; she proved most scornfully
I asked her for to marry, but she would not heed to me.
The night is almost spent, my love, it's near the break of day,
So now I want an answer; my dear, what do you say?

3 If I must tell you plainly, I'll lead a single life;
I never thought it suitable for me to be your wife;
So take this for an answer and for yourself provide,
For I've another more suitable, and you I'll lay aside.

4 Oh, you have stores of riches, and more you hope to gain,
And you have my fond wishes, but these you do disdain.
Your riches will not last you, they'll melt away like snow;
When poverty does cross you, you'll think of me, I know.

5 I'll steer my course for Flanders, I'll lead a single life,
And with my bold commander, my gun shall be my wife,
And when I do get money, to a tavern I will go,
And drink a health to Flora, although she answered no.

6 The small birds they are singing so sweetly and so fine;
My joys they would be springing if Flora was but mine;
But still this life is pleasant, and love must have its fill—
This world is wide and handsome: if you don't, some other will.

22 SHE'S LIKE THE SWALLOW

She's like the swal-low that flies so high, She's like the ri-ver that ne-ver runs dry, She's like the sun-shine on the lee shore. I love my love_ and love is no more.

1 She's like the swallow that flies so high,
   She's like the river that never runs dry,
   She's like the sunshine on the lee shore.
   I love my love and love is no more.

2 'Twas out in the garden this fair maid did go,
   A-picking the beautiful primerose;
   The more she plucked the more she pulled
   Until she got her aperon full.

3 It's out of those roses she made a bed,
   A stony pillow for her head.
   She laid her down, no word did say,
   Until this fair maid's heart did break.

4 She's like the swallow that flies so high,
   She's like the river that never runs dry,
   She's like the sunshine on the lee shore,
   I love my love and love is no more.

23 MARY ANN

Oh,— fare thee well, my own true love, Oh,— fare thee well, my dear,—— For the ship is a-wait-ing, the wind blows high, And I am bound a-way for the sea, Ma-ry Ann,—— And— I am bound a-way for the sea, Ma-ry Ann.

1 Oh, fare the well, my own true love,
Oh, fare thee well, my dear,
For the ship is a-waiting, the wind blows high,
And I am bound away for the sea, Mary Ann,
And I am bound away for the sea, Mary Ann.

2 Oh, yonder don't you see the dove
A-sitting on the stile?
She is mourning for the loss of her own true love
As I do now for you, my dear Mary Ann. (2)

3 A lobster boiling in the pot,
A blue-fish on the hook,
They are suffering long, but it's nothing like
The ache I bear for you, Mary Ann. (2)

4 Oh, had I but a flask of gin
With sugar here for two,
And a great big bowl for to mix it in,
I'd pour a drink for you, Mary Ann. (2)

24 THE LUMBER CAMP SONG

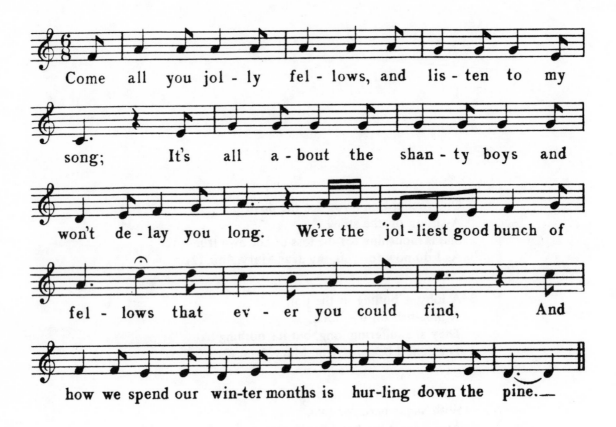

Come all you jol-ly fel-lows, and lis-ten to my song; It's all a-bout the shan-ty boys and won't de-lay you long. We're the 'jol-liest good bunch of fel-lows that ev-er you could find, And how we spend our win-ter months is hur-ling down the pine.__

1 Come all you jolly fellows, and listen to my song;
   It's all about the shanty boys and won't delay you long.
   We're the jolliest good bunch of fellows that ever you could find,
   And how we spend our winter months is hurling down the pine.

2 At four o'clock in the morning the boss he will shout:
   Heave out, my jolly teamsters; it's time to be on the route.
   The teamsters they jump up all in a frightened way:
   Where is me boots? Where is me pants? Me socks is gone astray.

CANADA

3 The next gets up is the choppers, whose socks they cannot find;
  They blames it on the teamsters and swear with all their mind.
  Some other man may have them on and he be standing near.
  Laugh it off all with a joke and have a hearty cheer.

4 At six o'clock it's breakfast and ev'ry man is out,
  And if a man he is not sick, he's sure to be on the route.
  There's sawyers and choppers to lay the timber low;
  There's swampers and loggers to drag it to and fro.

5 Crack! snack! goes my whip; I whistle and I sing;
  I sit upon my double sleigh as happy as a king.
  My horse is always ready, and I am never sad;
  There's no one else so happy as the double-sleigher lad.

6 The next comes is the loader, all at the break of day:
  Load up my slide, five hundred feet; to the river drive away.
  You can hear those axes ringing until the sun goes down.
  Hurrah, my boys! The day is spent. To the shanty we are boun .

7 We all arrive at the shanty, cold hands and wet feet.
  We there pull off our larrigans, our supper for to eat.
  We sing and dance till nine o'clock, then to our bunks we climb.
  Those winter months they won't be long in hurling down the pine.

8 The springtime rolls around, and the boss he will say:
  Heave down your saws and axes, b'ys, and help to clear away.
  The floating ice it is all gone and business is arrived;
  Two hundred able-bodied men is wanted on the drive.

9 The springtime rolls around, and glad will be the day
  When folks relate unto their friends, who wander back that way.
  So now my song is ended, and don't you think it's true?
  But if you doubt one word of it, just ask one of our crew.

UNITED STATES OF
AMERICA

25 THE WIFE OF USHER'S WELL

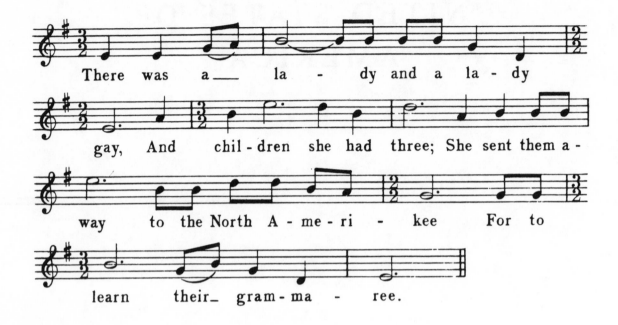

There was a___ la - dy and a la - dy gay, And chil - dren she had three; She sent them a - way to the North A - me - ri - kee For to learn their_ gram - ma - ree.

1 There was a lady and a lady gay,
   And children she had three;
   She sent them away to the North Amerikee
   For to learn their grammaree.

2 They hadn't been there very long,
   Scarce three months and a day,
   When death, sweet death came hastening along
   And took those babes away.

3 It was about old Christmas time,
   The nights being long and cold,
   When the lady spied her three little babes
   Come walking into the room.

4 She spread her table broad and wide;
  On it put bread and wine.
  Come eat, come drink, my sweet little babes.
  Come eat, come drink of mine.

5 We cannot eat your bread, mother,
  We cannot drink your wine,
  For yonder stands our Saviour so dear,
  To him we must return.

6 She put a bed in the backward room,
  And on it she put white sheets,
  On top of that a golden spread
  That they might the better sleep.

7 We cannot rest on your bed, mother,
  We cannot sleep on your sheets,
  For yonder stands our Saviour so dear,
  And we must rest at his feet.

8 Let's go, let's go, says the oldest one,
  For the chickens are crowing for day,
  And yonder stands our Saviour so dear,
  And we must fly away.

9 Marble stones at our heads, mother,
  Cold clay upon our feet;
  The tears that was shed over us last night
  Would have wet our winding sheet.

26 LITTLE MATTHY GROVES

On a high ho-li-day, on a high ho-li-day, The
ve-ry first day of the year, Lit-tle Mat-thy Groves to
church did go, God's ho-ly word to hear,_ hear, God's
ho - ly word to hear.

1 On a high holiday, on a high holiday,
The very first day of the year,
Little Matthy Groves to church did go
God's holy word to hear, hear,
God's holy word to hear.

2 The first that came in was a gay ladie,
And the next that came in was a girl,
And the next that came in was Lord
Arnold's wife,
The fairest of them all.

3 She stepped right up unto this one
And she made him this reply,
Saying: You must go home with me
tonight
All night with me for to lie.

4 I cannot go with you tonight,
I cannot for my life,
For I know by the rings that are on
your fingers
You are Lord Arnold's wife.

5 And if I am Lord Arnold's wife,
I know that Lord Arnold's gone away.
He's gone away to Old England
To see King Henery.

6 A little footpage was standing by,
And he took to his feet and run;
He run till he came to the waterside,
And he bent on his breast and swum.

7 What news, what news, my little
footpage,
What news have you for me?
Are my castle walls all torn down,
Or any of my men false be?

8 Your castle walls are not torn down
Nor any of your men false be,
But little Matthy Groves is in your house
In bed with your gay ladie!

UNITED STATES OF AMERICA

9 He took his merry men by the hand
And placed them all in a row,
And he bade them not one word for to
speak
And not one horn for to blow.

10 There was one man among them all
Who owed little Matthy some good will,
And he put his bugle horn to his mouth
And he blew both loud and shrill.

11 Hark, hark! hark, hark! said little
Matthy Groves,
I hear the bugle blow,
And every note it seems to say
Arise, arise and go!

12 Lie down, lie down, little Matthy
Groves,
And keep my back from the cold;
It is my father's shepherd boys
A-blowing up the sheep from the fold.

13 From that they fell to hugging and
kissing
And from that they fell to sleep;
And next morning when they woke at
the break of day
Lord Arnold stood at their feet.

14 And it's how do you like my fine
featherbed,
And it's how do you like my sheets?
And it's how do you like my gay ladie
That lies in your arms and sleeps?

15 Very well do I like your fine featherbed,
Very well do I like your sheets;
But much better do I like your gay
ladie
That lies in my arms and sleeps.

16 Now get you up, little Matthy Groves,
And all your clothes put on;
For it never shall be said in Old England
That I slew a naked man.

17 I will get up, said little Matthy Groves,
And fight you for my life,
Though you've two bright swords
hanging by your side
And me not a pocket knife.

18 If I've two bright swords by my side,
They cost me deep in purse,
And you shall have the better of the two
And I will keep the worse.

19 The very first lick that little Matthy
struck
He wounded Lord Arnold sore.
But the very first lick that Lord Arnold
struck
Little Matthy struck no more.

20 He took his lady by the hand
And he downed her on his knee,
Saying: Which do you like the best, my
dear,
Little Matthy or me?

21 Very well do I like your rosy cheeks,
Very well do I like your dimpled chin,
But better do I like little Matthy Groves
Than you and all your kin.

22 He took his lady by the hand
And led her o'er the plain;
He took the broad sword from his side
And he split her head in twain.

23 Hark, hark, hark, doth the nightingale sing,
And the sparrows they do cry;
Today I've killed two true lovers,
And tomorrow I must die!

27 THE HOUSE CARPENTER

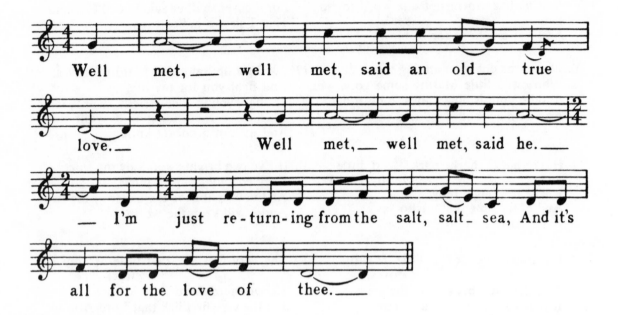

Well met, __ well met, said an old __ true love. __ Well met, __ well met, said he. __ __ I'm just re-turn-ing from the salt, salt __ sea, And it's all for the love of thee. __

1 Well met, well met, said an old true love.
  Well met, well met, said he.
  I'm just returning from the salt, salt sea,
  And it's all for the love of thee.

2 Come in, come in, my old true love,
  And have a seat with me.
  It's been three-fourths of a long, long year
  Since together we have been.

3 Well, I can't come in and I can't sit down
  For I haven't but a moment's time.
  They say you're married to a house carpenter,
  And your heart will never be mine.

4 Now, it's I could have married a king's daughter dear
  – I'm sure she'd have married me –
  But I've forsaken her crowns of gold,
  And it's all for the love of thee.

5 Now, will you forsake your house carpenter,
  And go along with mè?
  I'll take you where the grass grows green
  On the banks of the deep blue sea.

6 She picked up her little babe,
  And kisses gave it three.
  Says: Stay right here, my darling little babe,
  And keep your papa company.

7 She dressed herself in scarlet red,
  Put on a sash of green,
  And over the streets as she passed by
  She shone like a glittering queen.

8 Well, they hadn't been on ship but about two weeks,
  I'm sure it was not three,
  Till his true love she began to mourn,
  And she weeped most bitterly.

9 Says: Are you a-weeping for my silver and my gold?
  Says: Are you a-weeping for my store?
  Or are you weeping for that house carpenter
  Whose face you'll never see any more?

10 No, it's I'm not a-weeping for your silver and your gold,
  Or neither for your store.
  I am a-weeping for my dear little babe
  Whose face I'll never see any more.

11 Well, they hadn't been a-sailing but about three weeks,
  I'm sure it was not four,
  Till they sprung a leak in the bottom of the ship,
  And it sunken for to rise no more.

28 MR. WOODBURY'S COURTSHIP

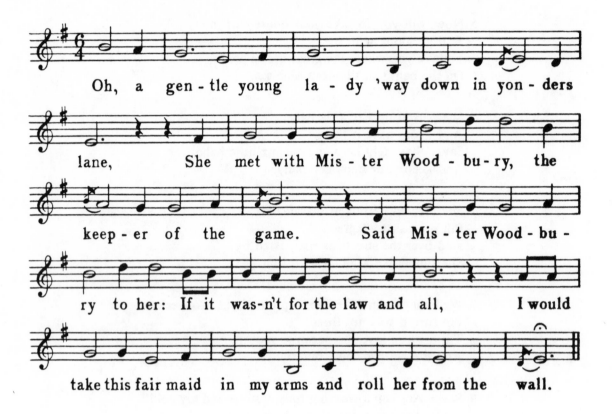

Oh, a gen-tle young la-dy 'way down in yon-ders lane, She met with Mis-ter Wood-bu-ry, the keep-er of the game. Said Mis-ter Wood-bu-ry to her: If it was-n't for the law and all, I would take this fair maid in my arms and roll her from the wall.

1 Oh, a gentle young lady 'way down in yonders lane,
  She met with Mister Woodbury, the keeper of the game.
  Said Mister Woodbury to her: If it wasn't for the law and all,
  I would take this fair maid in my arms and roll her from the wall.

2 – Oh, go away, you foolish man, and don't you bother me.
  Before you and I in one bed lie, you cook me dishes three.
  Three dishes you will cook for me, and I will eat them all,
  Before you and I in one bed lie, and I lie next the wall.

3 For my breakfast, you cook for me a cherry without a stone;
  For my dinner, you will cook for me a bird that has no bone;
  For my supper, you will fry me a bird that has no gall,
  Before you and I in one bed lie, and I lie next the wall.

4 -- Oh, a cherry when it's in blossom, it hasn't any stone;
A chicken when in a egg, I know it has no bone;
The dove she is a gentle bird, she flies without a gall;
So jump into my arms, my love, and I'll roll you from the wall.

5 - Oh, go away, you foolish man, before you me perplex.
Before you and I in one bed lie, you answer questions six.
- Six questions you will give to me, and I will name them all,
Before you and I in one bed lie, and you lie next the wall.

6 - What rounder is than my gold ring, what's deeper than the sea,
What is worse than a woman's tongue, what's higher than a tree,
What bird sings first, and which one best, and where does the dew first fall?
Before you and I in one bed lie, and I lie next the wall.

7 -Oh, this globe is rounder than your gold ring, hell's deeper than the sea,
The devil is worse than a woman's tongue, heaven's higher than the tree,
The lark sings first and likewise best, on the treetops dew first falls,
So jump into my arms, my love, and I'll roll you from the wall.

8 - Oh, go away, you foolish man, and don't you bother me.
Before you and I in one bed lie, you get me articles three.
Three articles you will get for me, and I will use them all,
Before you and I in one bed lie, and I lie next the wall.

9 First I want some foreign fruit that in Car'lina grew;
Next I want a silk dolman that never a warp went through;
Next I want a sparrow's thorn, it will do us one and all,
Before you and I in one bed lie, and I'll lie next the wall.

10 - Oh, my father has some foreign fruit that in Car'lina grew;
My mother has a silk dolman that never a warp went through;
The sparrow's thorns are easy found, there's one for every claw.
So he took the fair maid in his arms, and rolled her next the wall.

29   THE GALLOWS TREE

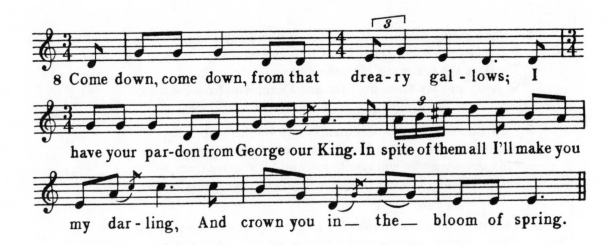

8 Come down, come down, from that drea-ry gal-lows; I
have your par-don from George our King. In spite of them all I'll make you
my dar-ling, And crown you in— the— bloom of spring.

1 My love he was as fine a fellow
As ever nature formed or the sun shone on,
And how to gain him I do not know,
For I hear his sentence is to be hung.

2 As I was walking the streets of Derry,
His charming features I chanced to espy;
He looked more like some commanding officer
Than any young man condemned to die.

3 When he got to the first step of the gallows,
His own father he chanced to see.
Step up, step up, my beloved father,
I have one word to exchange with thee.

4 Where is my true love, oh, where is my jewel,
That she don't come and visit me?
Or does she think it a shame or a scandal
To see me die on the gallows tree?

5 When he got to the second step of the gallows,
His own dear sister by chance he did see.
Step up, step up, my beloved sister,
I have one word to exchange with thee.

6 He took a gold ring off from his finger,
And wrapped it in her silk so fine.
Take this, take this, my beloved sister,
And keep your brother close in your mind.

7 And when he got to the top of the gallows
His own dear sweetheart by chance he did see,
Riding in a coach that was lined with linen,
So swift she rode and swift rode she.

8 Come down, come down, from that dreary gallows;
I have your pardon from George our King.
In spite of them all I'll make you my darling.
And crown you in the bloom of spring.

30 THE LOW-DOWN LONESOME LOW

1 Captain, O captain, what will you give me
  If I will sink the *Turkey Reveille,*
  As she sails in the low-down,
  Low-down, low-down,
  As she sails in the low-down, lonesome low?

2 Gold and silver, shining so bright
  And my fairest daughter shall wed you tonight,
  If you sink her in the low-down,
  Low-down, low-down,
  If you sink her in the low-down lonesome low.

3 Then he bared his breast and he swam
                          on the sea
  Till he came along by the *Turkey
                          Reveille*
  As she sailed in the low-down,
  Low-down, low-down,
  As she sailed in the low-down, lonesome
                          low.

4 Some with their cards and some with
                          their dice,
  And some were taking their best friend's
                          advice,
  As she rowed in the low-down,
  Low-down, low-down,
  As she rowed in the low-down, lonesome
                          low.

5 Then he bared his breast and he swam
                          in the tide,
  And bored ten holes in the old ship's
                          side,
  And she sank in the low-down,
  Low-down, low-down,
  And she sank in the low-down, lonesome
                          low.

6 Some with their hats and some with
                          their caps
  Were trying to stop them salt-water
                          gaps,
  As she sailed in the low-down,
  Low-down, low-down,
  As she sailed in the low-down, lonesome
                          low.

7 Then he bared his breast and he swam in
                          the tide
  Until he come along by his own ship's
                          side,
  As she rolled in the low-down,
  Low-down, low-down,
  As she rolled in the low-down, lonesome
                          low.

8 Captain, oh, captain, take me on board,
  For if you don't you have forfeited your
                          word,
  As you sail in the low-down,
  Low-down, low-down,
  As you sail in the low-down, lonesome
                          low.

9 Sailor boy, sailor boy, don't appeal to
                          me,
  For you drowned fifty souls when you
                          sank the *Reveille,*
  As she sailed in the low-down,
  Low-down, low-down,
  As she sailed in the low-down, lonesome
                          low.

10 If it wasn't for the love that I have for
                          your men,
   I would serve you the same as I've
                          served them,
   As you sail in the low-down,
   Low-down, low-down,
   As you sail in the low-down, lonesome
                          low.

11 Then he hoisted his sails, and away
                          sailed he,
   And he left the poor sailor boy to drown
                          in the sea,
   To drown in the low-down,
   Low-down, low-down,
   To drown in the low-down, lonesome
                          low.

12 So he bared his breast and down swam
                          he,
   He swam till he came to the bottom of
                          the sea,
   And he drowned in the low-down,
   Low-down, low-down,
   And he drowned in the low-down,
                          lonesome low.

31 LOCKS AND BOLTS

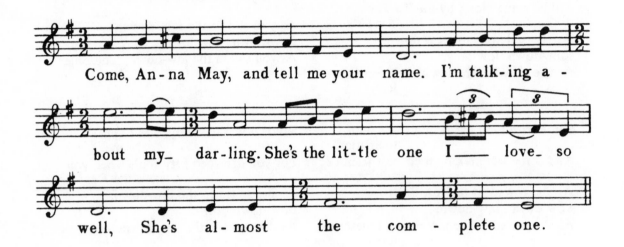

Come, An-na May, and tell me your name. I'm talk-ing a-bout my_ dar-ling. She's the lit-tle one I___ love_ so well, She's al-most the com - plete one.

1 Come, Anna May, and tell me your
                                      name.
I'm talking about my darling.
She's the little one I love so well,
She's almost the complete one.

2 Her yellow hairs, like glittering gold,
Come jingling down her pillow.
She's the little one I love so well,
She's like the weeping willow.

3 You've caused your parents to owe me
                                    a grudge
And treat me most unkindly,
Because you're of some high degree
And me so poor and needy.

4 I went up to her uncle's house,
Enquiring of my darling;
And all they would say: There's no
                                such here.
And then O what weeping!

5 But when she heard my lonely voice,
She answered at the window,
Saying: I would be with you soon, my
                                      love,
But locks and bolts doth hinder.

6 I stood for a moment all in a maze,
I viewed her long and tenderly;
My spirit flew, my sword I drew,
I swore that house I'd enter.

7 The blood was shed from every side
Till I got her from among them.
And all young men who get such wives
Should fight till you overcome them.

32 THE NIGHTINGALE

One morn-ing, one morn-ing, one morn-ing in May, I
met a fair cou-ple a-mak-ing their way;
One was a la-dy, so neat and so fair, The
o-ther a sol-dier, a brave vo-lun-teer.

1 One morning, one morning, one morning in May,
I met a fair couple a-making their way;
One was a lady, so neat and so fair,
The other a soldier, a brave volunteer.

2 Good morning, good morning, good morning to thee.
Now where are you going, my pretty lady?
I'm a-going a-walking to the banks of the sea
To see the waters a-gliding and hear the nightingales sing.

3 They hadn't been standing but one hour or two
Till out of his knapsack his fiddle he drew,
And the tune that he played made the valleys to ring.
See the waters a-gliding and hear the nightingales sing.

4 Pretty lady, pretty lady, 'tis time to give o'er.
O no, pretty soldier, please play one tune more.
I'd rather hear your fiddle by the touch of one string
Than see the waters a-gliding and hear the nightingales sing.

5 Then, pretty soldier, will you marry me?
O no, pretty lady, that never can be;
I have a wife in London and children twice three,
Two wives in the army is too many for me.

6 I'll go back to London and stay there one year
And drink all my living in whisky and beer;
And if ever I return it will be in the Spring.
See the waters a-gliding and hear the nightingale sing.

33 JACKIE FRAZIER

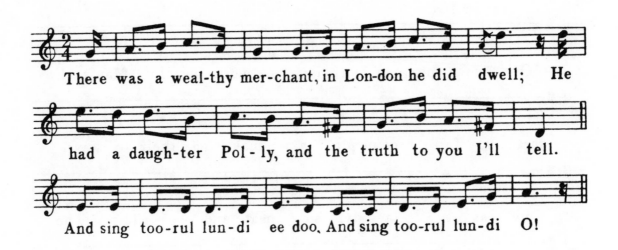

There was a weal-thy mer-chant, in Lon-don he did dwell; He
had a daugh-ter Pol-ly, and the truth to you I'll tell.
And sing too-rul lun-di ee doo, And sing too-rul lun-di O!

1 There was a wealthy merchant, in London he did dwell;
  He had a daughter Polly, and the truth to you I'll tell.
      And sing toorul lundi ee doo,
      And sing toorul lundi O!

2 She had both lords and squires, and courted day and night,
  But on none but Jack her sailor boy she placed her heart's delight.

3 Her father being in a passion, and unto her did say:
  Good morning, Madam Frazier, since that's your truelove's name!

4 Father, here is my body, and it you may confine,
  But none but Jack the sailor boy can ever suit my mind.

5 Polly being at liberty, and money at command,
  She took a sudden notion to see some foreign land.

6 She went into a tailor's shop and dressed in men's array,
  And bargained with her sailor boy to carry her away.

7 It's now you are on shipboard, your name I wish to know,
  She, smiling in her countenance: They call me Jack Monroe.

8 It's now they have anchored and sailed far away.
They landed at French Landing on a clear and pleasant day.

9 Your waist it is too slender, your hands they are too small,
Your cheeks they are too rosy red to face the cannon ball.

10 I know my waist is slender, my hands they are but small;
But my cheeks are not too rosy red to face the cannon ball!

11 So the drums did beat and rattle, and the fife did sweetly play;
She marched up to the enemy and bravely fought away.

12 The drums did beat and rattle, and the cannon balls did fly,
When a ball from the enemy caused her darling down to lie.

13 She picked him up in her own arms, and carried him to the town,
And left him with a surgeon to heal his bleeding wounds.

14 So now the war is over, and they'll sail back again;
They landed at her father's house on a clear and pleasant morn.

15 Her mother being near them, and in some secret place,
Says she: This young man's features resemble Polly's face!

16 I am your daughter Polly, from you I run away;
I followed Jack my sailor boy to the wars of Germany.

17 I followed him over land, and I followed him over sea;
I married him in the army, and I have him here with me.

18 So come all ye tender parents, and never part true love,
For you're bound to see in some degree the ruin it will prove.

19 So now they are both married and living at their ease;
So, parents, let your children get married as they please.
  And sing toorul lundi ee doo
  And sing toorul lundi O!

34 DANIEL MONROE

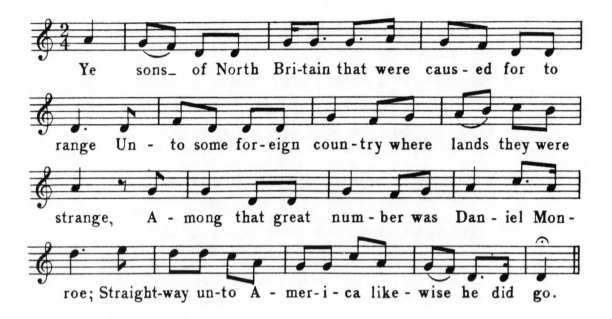

Ye sons_ of North Bri-tain that were caus-ed for to range Un - to some for-eign coun-try where lands they were strange, A - mong that great num-ber was Dan - iel Mon - roe; Straight-way un-to A - mer-i-ca like-wise he did go.

1 Ye sons of North Britain that were caused for to range
Unto some foreign country where lands they were strange.
Among that great number was Daniel Monroe;
Straightway unto America likewise he did go.

2 Two sons with his brother he caused them to stay.
The price of their passage he could not well pay.
When seven long winters had passed by and gone,
They asked for to leave, but money was none.

3 Being discontented, no comfort they find,
But the thoughts of the army did run in their mind:
So leaving their uncle, they roamed till they found
A regiment of foot for America bound.

4 And when they had landed in that country wild,
Surrounded by rebels on every side,
With humb'e submission these two brothers went
Unto their good captain to gain his consent.

5 To which their good captain was pleased to agree
  They might go up-country their parents to see.
  So leaving the camp with a boy for a guide,
  They made for the place where their parents reside.

6 They travelled along till they came to a grove.
  The leaves and the branches they all seemed to move:
  There being two rebels that lurked in the wood,
  They pointed their pistols where the two brothers stood.

7 Lodging a bullet in each brother's breast,
  They rushed on their prey like two ravenous beasts,
  To take all their money and rip up their clothes,
  And if they're not dead, for to give them some blows.

8 You ravenous villains, you bloodthirsty hounds,
  How could you have killed us before we had found,
  Had found our dear father we sought with such care?
  When he hears of our fate he will die of despair.

9 He left us in Scotland seven twelvemonths ago.
  Perhaps you may know him, his name is Monroe.
  The old man astonished, in wonder he stood
  A-gazing on his sons who lay bleeding in the wood.

10 He cried out in sorrow: Oh, what have I done?
   A curse on my hands, I have slain my own son!
   If you be my father, the young man did cry,
   I'm glad that I've seen you before that I die.

11 I'll sink beneath sorrow, give way to despair.
   I'll linger a while till death ends my care,
   In hopes for to meet you on a happier shore
   Where I won't be able to kill you any more.

35 THE PINERY BOY

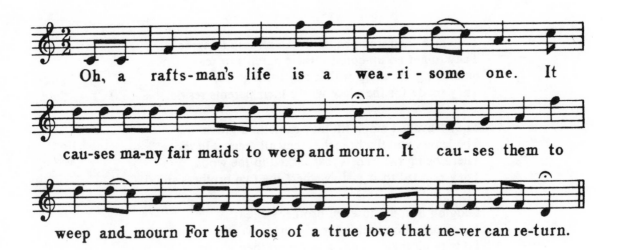

Oh, a rafts-man's life is a wea-ri-some one. It cau-ses ma-ny fair maids to weep and mourn. It cau-ses them to weep and mourn For the loss of a true love that ne-ver can re-turn.

1 Oh, a raftsman's life is a wearisome one.
It causes many fair maids to weep and
mourn.
It causes them to weep and mourn
For the loss of a true love that never can
return.

2 O father, O father, build me a boat,
That down the Wisconsin I may float,
And every raft that I pass by
There I will inquire for my sweet Pinery
Boy.

3 As she was rowing down the stream,
She saw three rafts all in a string.
She hailed the pilot as they drew nigh,
And there she did inquire for her sweet
Pinery Boy.

4 O pilot, O pilot, tell me true,
Is my sweet Willie among your crew?
Oh, tell me quick and give me joy,
For none other will I have but my sweet
Pinery Boy.

5 Oh, auburn was the colour of his hair.
His eyes were blue and his cheeks were
fair.
His lips were of a ruby fine;
Ten thousand times they've met with
mine.

6 O honoured lady, he is not here.
He's drowned in the dells, I fear.
'Twas at Lone Rock as we passed by,
Oh, there is where we left your sweet
Pinery Boy.

7 She wrung her hands and tore her hair,
Just like a lady in great despair.
She rowed her boat against Lone Rock.
You'd a-thought this fair lady's heart was
broke.

8 Dig me a grave both long and deep,
Place a marble slab at my head and feet;
And on my breast a turtle dove
To let the world know that I died for
love;
And at my feet a spreading oak
To let the world know that my heart was
broke.

36 THE DEAR COMPANION

I once did have a dear com-pan-ion; In-deed, I
thought his love my own, Un-til a black-eyed girl betrayed me, And then he cares no__ more for me.

1 I once did have a dear companion;
  Indeed, I thought his love my own,
  Until a black-eyed girl betrayed me,
  And then he cares no more for me.

2 Just go and leave me if you wish to;
  It will never trouble me,
  For in your heart you love another,
  And in my grave I'd rather die.

3 Last night while you were sweetly sleeping,
  Dreaming of some sweet repose,
  While me a poor girl broken, broken hearted,
  Listen to the wind that blows.

4 When I see your babe a-laughing
  It makes me think of your sweet face,
  But when I see your babe a-crying
  It makes me think of my disgrace.

37   BLACK IS THE COLOUR

But black is the col-our of my true love's hair, His face is
like some ro - sy fair; The pret-tiest face and the neat-est
hands, I love the ground_ where-on he stands.

1 But black is the colour of my true love's hair,
His face is like some rosy fair;
The prettiest face and the neatest hands,
I love the ground whereon he stands.

2 I love my love and well he knows
I love the ground whereon he goes.
If you no more on earth I see,
I can't serve you as you have me.

3 The winter's passed and the leaves are green,
The time is passed that we have seen,
But still I hope the time will come
When you and I shall be as one.

4 I go to the Clyde for to mourn and weep,
But satisfied I never could sleep.
I'll write you in a few short lines,
I'll suffer death ten thousand times.

5 I love my love and well he knows,
I love the ground whereon he goes;
The prettiest face, the neatest hands,
I love the ground whereon he stands.

38 WHEN FIRST TO THIS COUNTRY A STRANGER I CAME

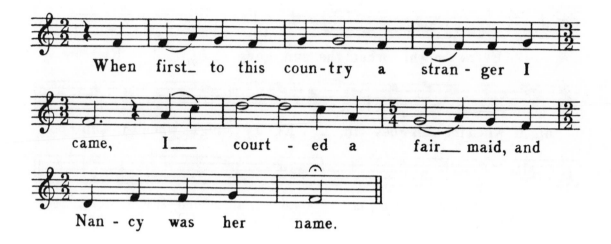

When first to this country a stranger I came, I courted a fair maid, and Nancy was her name.

1 When first to this country a stranger I came,
  I courted a fair maid, and Nancy was her name.

2 I courted her for love, her love I didn't obtain;
  Do you think I've any reason or right to complain?

3 I rode to see my Nancy, the pride of my life;
  I courted dearest Nancy, my own heart's true delight.

4 I rode to see my Nancy, I rode both day and night,
  Till I saw a fine gray horse, both plump-looking and white.

5 The sheriff's men, they followed and overtaken me,
  They carted me away to the penitentiary.

6 They opened the door and then they shoved me in,
  They shaved my head and cleared off my chin.

7 They beat me and they banged me, they fed me on dry beans,
  Till I wished to my own soul I'd never been a thief.

8 With my hands in my pockets, my cap put on so bold,
  With my coat of many colours, like Jacob's of old.

39 EVERY NIGHT WHEN THE SUN GOES IN

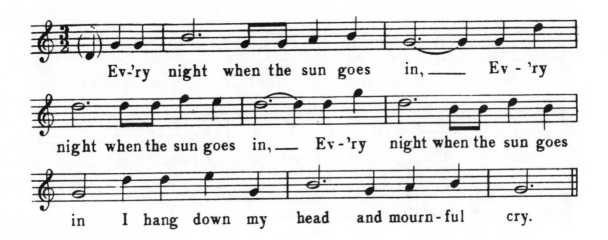

Ev-'ry night when the sun goes in, ___ Ev - 'ry night when the sun goes in, ___ Ev -'ry night when the sun goes in I hang down my head and mourn-ful cry.

1 Every night when the sun goes in,
Every night when the sun goes in,
Every night when the sun goes in
I hang down my head and mournful cry.
    True love, don't weep, true love, don't mourn,
    True love, don't weep, true love don't mourn,
    True love don't weep nor mourn for me,
    I'm going away to Marble town.

2 I wish to the Lord that train would come (3)
To take me back where I come from.

3 It's once my apron hung down low, (3)
He'd follow me through both sleet and snow.

4 It's now my apron's to my chin, (3)
He'll face my door and won't come in.

5 I wish to the Lord my babe was born,
A-sitting upon his pappy's knee,
And me, poor girl, was dead and gone,
And the green grass growing over me.
    True love, don't weep, true love don't mourn,
    True love don't weep, true love don't mourn,
    True love don't weep nor mourn for me,
    I'm going away to Marble town.

40 PRETTY SARO

When I first came to this coun-try in eigh-teen and for-ty-nine, I saw ma-ny fair lo-vers, but I ne-ver saw mine; I view it all a-round me, I found my-self lone, And me a poor stran-ger and a long way from home.

1 When I first came to this country in eighteen and fortynine,
I saw many fair lovers, but I never saw mine;
I view it all around me, I found myself lone,
And me a poor stranger and a long way from home.

2 My love she won't love me, yes, I do understand,
She wants a freeholder and I've got no land,
But plenty to maintain her on, silver and gold,
And as many other fine things as my love's house can hold.

3 Farewell to my mother and adieu to my old father, too,
I am going to ramble this whole world all through;
And when get tired I'll set down and weep
And think of my darling, pretty Saro, my sweet.

4 Down in some lonesome valley, down in some lone place,
Where the small birds do whistle their notes to increase;
But when I get sorrow, I'll set down and cry
And think of my darling, my darling so nigh.

5 I wish I were a poet and could write some fine hand,
I would write my love a letter that she might understand;
I would send it by the water where the island overflow,
And I'd think of my darling wherever I go.

6 I wish I were a dove and had wings and could fly;
This night to my love's window I would draw nigh,
And in her lily-white arms all night I would lay
And watch them little windows to the dawning of day.

41 THE CHICKENS THEY ARE CROWING

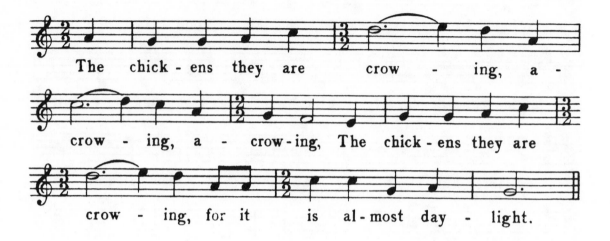

1 The chickens they are crowing, a-crowing, a-crowing,
  The chickens they are crowing, for it is almost daylight.

2 My mother she will scold me, will scold me, will scold me,
  My mother she will scold me for staying away all night.

3 My father he'll uphold me, uphold me, uphold me,
  My father he'll uphold me and say I'd a-done just right.

4 I won't go home till morning, till morning, till morning,
  I won't go home till morning, and I'll stay with the girls all night.

5 The chickens they are crowing, a-crowing, a-crowing,
  The chickens they are crowing, for it is almost daylight.

42 SALLY BUCK

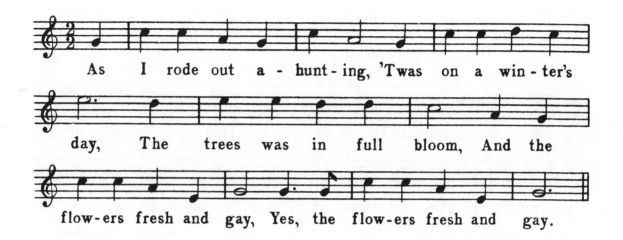

As I rode out a-hunt-ing, 'Twas on a win-ter's day, The trees was in full bloom, And the flow-ers fresh and gay, Yes, the flow-ers fresh and gay.

1 As I rode out a-hunting,
  'Twas on a winter's day,
  The trees was in full bloom,
  And the flowers fresh and gay,
    Yes, the flowers fresh and gay.

2 As I went out a-hunting
  I rode down on the river brim,
  And there I spied a thousand deer
  All on the tide did swim.

3 I cocked my gun immediately
  And under water went;
  For to kill one of them deers
  It was my whole intent.

4 I being under water,
  Ten thousand feet or more,
  I fired off my pistol,
  Like cannons they did roar.

5 I killed one of them deer
  And out of water went;
  For to seek for those that fled
  It was my whole intent.

6 I bent my gun in a circle
  And shot all round the hill,
  And out of five-and-twenty deer
  Ten thousand I did kill.

7 And as I stood there a-gazing
  I saw the moon draw nigh;
  And I clapped my wings upon my back,
  Hopped on as she passed by.

8 And as the moon went down at night
  She fetched a certain whirl;
  And that's the way this poor boy
  Fell into the world.

9 The money that I got
  For my meat and skin,
  I put in a forty foot barn
  And it would not all go in.

10 The balance of my money
  I lent it out of hand,
  And now intend to live
  A jolly, jolly gentleman,
    Yes, a jolly, jolly gentleman.

43 SWING A LADY ROUND

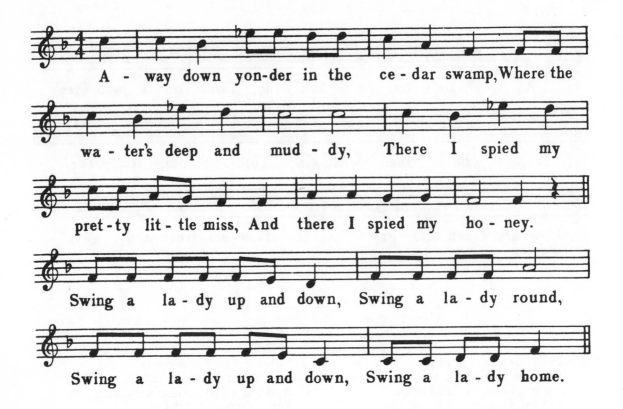

A - way down yon-der in the ce - dar swamp, Where the wa - ter's deep and mud - dy, There I spied my pret - ty lit - tle miss, And there I spied my ho - ney.

Swing a la - dy up and down, Swing a la - dy round, Swing a la - dy up and down, Swing a la - dy home.

1 Away down yonder in the cedar swamp,
Where the water's deep and muddy,
There I spied my pretty little miss,
And there I spied my honey.
    Swing a lady up and down,
    Swing a lady round,
    Swing a lady up and down,
    Swing a lady home.

2 Build my wife a fine brick house,
Build it in the garden,
And if you don't mind, she'll jump out,
So fare you well, my darling.

3 The love of one is better than none,
The love of two is a-plenty,
The love of three it can't agree,
You'd better not love so many.

4 The blue-eyed boy's gone back on me,
The brown-eyed boy won't marry;
Before I'd take the cross-eyed boy,
An old-maid-life I'd tarry.
    Swing a lady up and down,
    Swing a lady round,
    Swing a lady up and down,
    Swing a lady home.

44 LIZA ANNE

Works my hor-ses in my team, And I work old grey be-fore. Pret-ty near broke my true love's heart To hear the ban-jo roar.

1 Works my horses in my team,
And I work old grey before.
Pretty near broke my true love's heart
To hear the banjo roar.

2 Set my mill a-grinding;
She ground all sorts of grain,
She ground just thirty-nine bushels
Without a drop of rain.

3 Preacher's in the pulpit
Preaching mighty bold;
He's a-preaching for the money,
But not to save no soul.

4 Beefsteak when I'm hungry,
And whisky when I'm dry;
Greenback for to carry me through,
And heaven when I die.

5 Bob he'll ride the old grey horse
And Calamy rides the bay;
Bob he drinks the buttermilk
While Calamy drinks the whey.

6 Set my mill a-grinding,
And the water poured over the dam.
Thought I'd make a fortune
By marrying Liza Anne.

7 Rabbit in the lowlands
Scratching in the sand.
I bet you before tomorrow night
I'll be some pretty girl's man.

8 Rabbit in the 'simmon tree,
Possum's on the ground.
Possum says: You big-eyed brute,
Shake the 'simmon down.

9 Called my wife a nigger,
But she's neither black nor brown;
She's just the colour of a thunder-cloud
Just before the rain pours down.

10 You ride the old grey horse
And I'll ride the roan.
You talk to your true love
And just let mine alone.

45 MAMMA'S GONE TO THE MAIL BOAT

1 Bye-o, baby, bye,
  Bye-o, baby, bye,
  Mamma's gone to the mail boat,
  Mamma's gone to the mail boat,
  Bye.

2 Go to sleepy, baby, bye,
  Go to sleepy, baby, bye,
  Father's gone to the mail boat.
  Father's gone to the mail boat,
  Bye.

46 THE LAZY FARMER

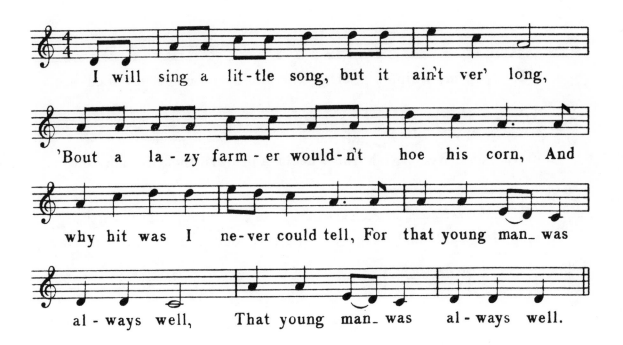

I will sing a lit-tle song, but it ain't ver' long,

'Bout a la-zy farm-er would-n't hoe his corn, And

why hit was I ne-ver could tell, For that young man_ was

al-ways well, That young man_ was al-ways well.

1 I will sing a little song, but it ain't ver'
                long,
 'Bout a lazy farmer wouldn't hoe his corn,
 And why hit was I never could tell,
 For that young man was always well,
 That young man was always well.

2 He planted his corn on June the last.
 In July it was up to his eye.
 In September there came a big frost,
 And all that young man's corn was lost.

3 He start to the field and he got there at
                last.
 The grass and the weeds was up to his
                chin.
 The grass and the weeds had grown so
                high,
 Caused that poor man for to sigh.

4 Now, his courtship had just begun;
 Saying: Young man, have you hoed your
                corn?
 I've tried, I've tried, but all in vain,
 For I don't believe I'll raise one grain.

5 Why do you come to me to wed
 If you can't raise your own corn-bread?
 Single I am and will remain,
 For a lazy man I won't maintain.

6 He hung his head and walked away,
 Saying: Kind miss, you'll rue the day,
 You'll rue the day that you was born
 For giving me the devil 'case I wouldn't
                hoe my corn.

7 Now his courtship was to an end,
 On his way he then began,
 Saying: Kind miss, I'll have another girl
 If I have to ramble this big wide world,
 If I have to ramble this big wide world.

47 OX-DRIVING SONG

I pop my whip, I bring the blood, I make my lead-ers take the mud, We grab the wheels and turn them round; One long, long pull and we're on hard ground.__ To my rol, to rol, to my ri - de - o, To my rol, to rol, to my ri - de - o, To my ri - de - o, to my ru - de - o, To my rol, to my rol, to my ri - de - o.__

1 I pop my whip, I bring the blood,
   I make my leaders take the mud,
   We grab the wheels and turn them round;
   One long, long pull and we're on hard ground.
      To my rol, to rol, to my rideo,
      To my rol, to rol, to my rideo,
      To my rideo, to my rudeo,
      To my rol, to my rol, to my rideo.

2 On the fourteenth day of October-o,
  I hitched my team in order-o,
  To drive the hills of Salud-i-o,
  To my rol, to my rol, to my rideo.

3 When I got there the hills were steep,
  'Twould make any tender-hearted person weep
  To hear me cuss and pop my whip,
  To see my oxen pull and slip.

4 When I get home I'll have revenge;
  I'll land my family among my friends,
  I'll bid adieu to the whip and line
  And drive no more in the wintertime.
    To my rol, to rol, to my rideo,
    To my rideo, to my rudeo,
    To my rol, to rol, to my rideo,
    To my rol, to my rol, to my rideo.

48 THE BUFFALO SKINNERS

Come all you old-time cow-boys and lis-ten to my song. Please do not grow wea-ry, I'll not de-tain you long; Con-cern-ing some wild_ cow-boys who did a-gree_ to go, And spend a sum-mer plea-sant on the trail of the buf-fa - lo._

1 Come all you old-time cowboys and listen to my song.
   Please do not grow weary, I'll not detain you long;
   Concerning some wild cowboys who did agree to go,
   And spend a summer pleasant on the trail of the buffalo.

2 I found myself in Griffin in the Spring of '83,
   When a well-known, famous drover come a-walking up to me,
   Saying: How do you do, young feller, and how would you like to go,
   And spend a summer pleasant on the trail of the buffalo?

3 Well, me being out of work right then, to the drover I did say:
This going out on the buffalo range depends upon your pay.
But if you will pay good wages, transportation to and fro,
I think I might go with you to the trail of the buffalo.

4 Of course I'll pay good wages, give transportation too,
If you'll agree to work for me until the season's through.
But if you do grow weary, and you try to run away,
You'll starve to death along the trail, and also lose your pay.

5 Well, with all his flattering talking, he signed up quite a train,
Some ten or twelve in number, some able-bodied men.
Our trip it was a pleasant one as we hit the westward road,
And crossed old Boggy Creek in old New Mexico.

6 There our pleasures ended and our troubles all begun.
A lightning storm did hit us, and made our cattle run.
Got all full of stickers from the cactus that did grow;
And outlaws waiting to pick us off in the hills of Mexico.

7 Well, the working season ended and the drover would not pay.
You all have drunk too much, you're all in debt to me.
But the cowboys never had heard of such a thing as a bankrupt law,
So we left that drover's bones to bleach on the trail of the buffalo.

49   THE DYING COWBOY

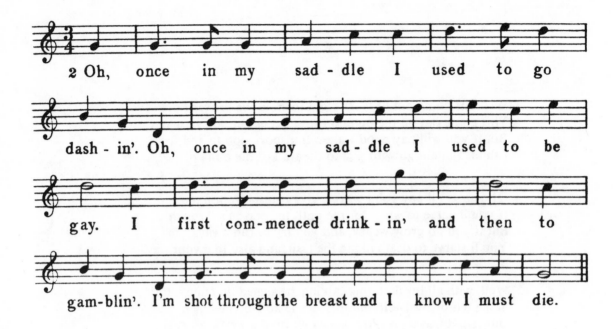

2 Oh, once in my sad - dle I used to go
dash - in'. Oh, once in my sad - dle I used to be
gay. I first com - menced drink - in' and then to
gam - blin'. I'm shot through the breast and I know I must die.

1 As I rode out by Tom Sherman's bar-room,
Tom Sherman's bar-room quite early one day,
I spied a young cowboy all dressed in white linen,
All dressed in white linen and fit for the grave.
    Oh, beat the drum slowly and play the fife lowly,
    Play the Dead March as you carry me along;
    Take me to the prairie and fire a volley o'er me,
    For I'm a young cowboy and dying alone.

2 Oh, once in my saddle I used to go dashin'.
Oh, once in my saddle I used to be gay.
I first commenced drinkin' and then to gamblin'.
I'm shot through the breast and I know I must die.

3 My lasso I used to throw to perfection,
A-ropin' wild cattle for me was great fun.
At punchin' I always have given satisfaction
With a bunch of wild cowboys, but now I am done.

4 Oh, bury me beside my knife and my shooter,
My spurs on my heels, my rifle by my side.
Over my coffin put a bottle of brandy,
That the cowboys may drink as they carry me along.

5 Go get six cowboys to carry my coffin,
Go get six pretty maidens to carry my pall.
Put bunches of roses all over my coffin,
Put roses to deaden the clods as they fall.

6 Go bring me a cup, a cup of cold water,
To cool my parched lips, the poor fellow said.
Before I had turned, the spirit had left him.
He had gone on a round-up and the cowboy was dead.
    We beat the drum slowly and played the fife lowly,
    We played the Dead March as we carried him along.
    We took him to the graveyard and threw the clods over him,
    For he was a young cowboy and he knew he'd done wrong.

50   RED IRON ORE

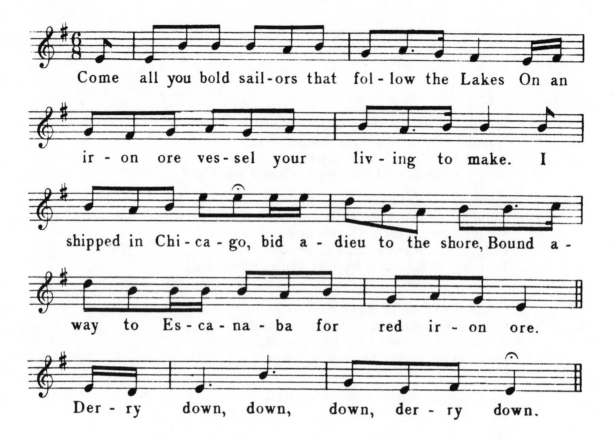

1 Come all you bold sailors that follow the Lakes
On an iron ore vessel your living to make.
I shipped in Chicago, bid adieu to the shore,
Bound away to Escanaba for red iron ore.
    Derry down, down, down, derry down.

2 In the month of September, the seventeenth day,
Two dollars and a quarter is all they would pay,
And on Monday morning the Bridgeport did take
The *E. C. Roberts* out in the Lake.

3 The wind from the south'ard sprang up a fresh breeze,
And away through Lake Michigan the *Roberts* did sneeze;
Down through Lake Michigan the *Roberts* did roar,
And on Friday morning we passed through death's door.

4 This packet she howled across the mouth of Green Bay,
   And before her cutwater she dashed the white spray.
   We rounded the sand point, our anchor let go,
   We furled in our canvas and the watch went below.

5 Next morning we hove alongside the Exile,
   And soon was made fast to an iron ore pile,
   They lowered their shutes and like thunder did roar,
   They spouted into us that red iron ore.

6 Some sailors took shovels, while others got spades,
   And some took wheelbarrows, – each man to his trade.
   We looked like red devils, our fingers got sore,
   We cursed Escanaba and that damned iron ore.

7 The tug *Escanaba* she towed out the Minch,
   The *Roberts* she thought she had left in a pinch,
   And as she passed by us she bid us good-bye,
   Saying: We'll meet you in Cleveland next Fourth of July!

8 Through Louse Island it blew a fresh breeze;
   We made the Foxes, the Beavers, the Skillagalees;
   We flew by the Minch for to show her the way,
   And she ne'er hove in sight till we were off Thunder Bay.

9 Across Saginaw Bay the *Roberts* did ride
   With the dark and deep water rolling over her side.
   And now for Port Huron the *Roberts* must go,
   Where the tug *Kate Williams* she took us in tow.

10 We went through North Passage – O Lord, how it blew!
   And all round the Dummy a large fleet there came too.
   The night being dark, Old Nick it would scare.
   We hove up next morning and for Cleveland did steer.

11 Now the *Roberts* is in Cleveland, made fast stem and stern,
   And over the bottle we'll spin a big yarn.
   But Captain Harvey Shannon had ought to stand treat
   For getting into Cleveland ahead of the fleet.

12 Now my song is ended, I hope you won't laugh.
   Our dunnage is packed and all hands are paid off.
   Here's a health to the *Roberts,* she's staunch, strong and true;
   Not forgetting the bold boys that comprise her crew.
     Derry down, down, down, derry down.

51 A SHANTY-MAN'S LIFE

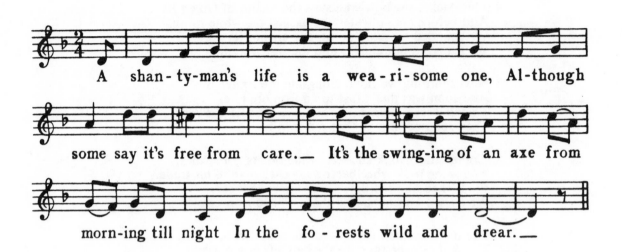

A shan-ty-man's life is a wea-ri-some one, Al-though
some say it's free from care.— It's the swing-ing of an axe from
morn-ing till night In the fo-rests wild and drear.—

1 A shanty-man's life is a wearisome one,
Although some say it's free from care.
It's the swinging of an axe from morning till night
In the forests wild and drear.

2 Or sleeping in the shanties dreary
When the winter winds do blow.
But as soon as the morning star does appear,
To the wild woods we must go.

3 At four in the morning our old greasy cook calls out:
Hurrah, boys, for it's day!
And from broken slumber we are aroused,
For to pass away the long winter's day.

4 Transported from the glass and the smiling little lass,
To the banks of some lonely stream,
Where the wolf, bear and owl with their terrifying howl
Disturb our nightly dreams.

5 When spring it does come in, double hardship then begins,
For the water is piercing cold;
Dripping wet will be our clothes and our limbs they are half-froze.
And our pike-poles we can scarcely hold.

6 Oh, the rocks, shoals and sands give employment to all hands,
As our well-bended raft we do steer,
And the rapids that we run, they seem to us but fun,
We're the boys free from slavish care.

7 Shantying I'll give o'er when I'm landed safe on shore,
And I'll lead a different life.
No longer will I roam, but contented stay at home,
With a pretty little smiling wife.

52 THE GREY GOOSE

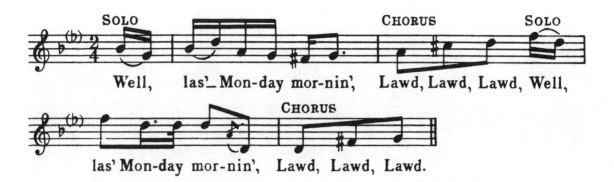

Well, las'_Mon-day mor-nin', Lawd, Lawd, Lawd, Well,

las' Mon-day mor-nin', Lawd, Lawd, Lawd.

1 Well, las' Monday mornin',
    Lawd, Lawd, Lawd,
Well, las' Monday mornin',
    Lawd, Lawd, Lawd.
My daddy went a-huntin'.
Well, he carried along his zulu.
Well, along come a grey goose.
Well, he throwed it to his shoulder,
An' he ram his hammer 'way back.
Well, he pulled on de trigger.
Well, down he come a-windin'.
He was six weeks a-fallin'.
He was six weeks a-findin'.
An' he put him on de wagon,
An' he taken him to de white house.
He was six weeks a-pickin'.
Lordy, your wife an' my wife,
Oh, dey give a feather pickin'.
An' dey put him on to parboil.
He was six months a-parboil',
An' dey put him on de table,
Now, de fork couldn' stick him,
An' de knife couldn't cut him.
An' dey throwed him in de hog-pen,
An' he broke de ol' sow's jaw-bone.
An' dey taken him to de saw-mill,
An' he broke de saw's teeth out.
An' de las' time I seed him,
Well, he's flyin' across de ocean,
Wid a long string o' goslin's,
An' dey all goin': Quank quink-quank,
    Lawd, Lawd, Lawd,
An' dey all goin': Quank quink-quank,
    Lawd, Lawd, Lawd.

53 MULE ON THE MOUNT

Cap-'n got a mule, mule on the Mount called Jer - ry, —

Cap-'n got a mule, mule on the Mount called Jer - ry, I can

ride, Lawd, — Lawd, I — can ride. —

1 Cap'n got a mule, mule on the Mount called Jerry,
Cap'n got a mule, mule on the Mount called Jerry,
I can ride, Lawd, Lawd, I can ride.

2 I don't want no cold corn bread and molasses,
I don't want no cold corn bread and molasses,
Gimme beans, Lawd, Lawd, gimme beans.

3 I don't want no coal-black woman for my regular,
I don't want no coal-black woman for my regular,
She's too low-down, Lawd, Lawd, she's too low-down.

4 I got a woman, she's got money 'cumulated,
I got a woman, she's got money 'cumulated,
In de bank, Lawd, Lawd, in de bank.

5 I got a woman she's pretty but she's too bulldozing,
I got a woman she's pretty but she's too bulldozing,
She won't live long, Lawd, Lawd, she won't live long.

6 Every pay day, pay day I gits a letter,
Every pay day, pay day I gits a letter,
Son come home, Lawd, Lawd, son come home.

7 If I can just make June, July and August,
If I can just make June, July and August,
I'm going home, Lawd, Lawd, I'm going home.

8 Don't you hear them coo-coo birds keep a'hollering,
Don't you hear them coo-coo birds keep a'hollering,
It's sign of rain, Lawd, Lawd, it's sign of rain.

9 I got a rainbow wrapped and tied around my shoulder,
I got a rainbow wrapped and tied around my shoulder,
It ain't goin' rain, Lawd, Lawd, it ain't goin' rain.

54 LYNCHBURG TOWN

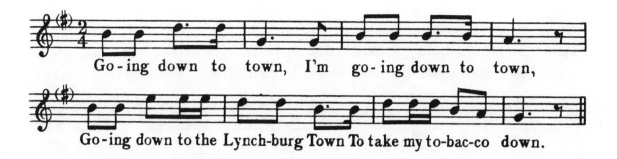

Go-ing down to town, I'm go-ing down to town,

Go-ing down to the Lynch-burg Town To take my to-bac-co down.

1 Going down to town,
  I'm going down to town,
  Going down to the Lynchburg Town
  To take my tobacco down.

2 Times a-getting hard,
  Money getting scarce.
  Pay me for them tobacco, boys,
  And I will leave this place.

3 Massa had an old grey horse,
  Took him down to town,
  Sold him for half a dollar
  And only a quarter down.

4 Old massa had a brand-new coat
  And he hung it on the wall.
  A nigger stole old massa's coat
  And wore it to the ball.

5 Old massa to the sheriff wrote
  And sent it by the mail.
  Mr Sheriff got old massa's note
  And put the thief in jail.

6 Old massa had a big brick house,
  'Twas sixteen storey's high,
  And every storey in that house
  Was full of chicken pie.

7 Old massa was a rich old man,
  He was richer than a king.
  He made me beat the old tin pan
  While Sary Jane would sing.

8 Going down to town,
  I'm going down to town,
  Going down to the Lynchburg Town
  To take my tobacco down.

9 Times a-getting hard,
  Money getting scarce.
  Pay me for them tobacco, boys,
  And I will leave this place.

55 THE BABE OF BETHLEHEM

Ye na-tions all,_ on you I call, come hear this de - clar-
a - tion, And don't re - fuse_ this glo - rious news of
Je - sus and_ sal - va - tion. To roy - al_ Jews came
first the_ news of Christ the great Mes - si - ah, As
was fore-told by pro-phets old, I - sai - ah, Je - re - mi - ah.

1 Ye nations all, on you I call, come hear this declaration,
   And don't refuse this glorious news of Jesus and salvation.
   To royal Jews came first the news of Christ the great Messiah,
   As was foretold by prophets old, Isaiah, Jeremiah.

2 To Abraham the promise came, and to his seed for ever,
   A light to shine in Isaac's line, by Scripture we discover;
   'Hail, promised morn! the Saviour's born, the glorious Mediator.
   God's blessed word made flesh and blood, assumed the human nature.

3 His parents poor in earthly store, to entertain the stranger
  They found no bed to lay his head, but in the ox's manger:
  No royal things, as used by kings, were seen by those that found him,
  But in the hay the stranger lay, with swaddling bands around him.

4 On the same night a glorious light to shepherds there appeared,
  Bright angels came in shining flame, they saw and greatly feared
  The angels said: Be not afraid, although we much alarm you,
  We do appear good news to bear, as now we will inform you.

5 The city's name is Bethlehem, in which God has appointed,
  This glorious morn a Saviour's born, for him God has anointed;
  By this you'll know, if you will go, to see this little stranger,
  His lovely charms in Mary's arms, both lying in a manger.

6 When this was said, straightway was made a glorious sound from heaven
  Each flaming tongue an anthem sung: To men a Saviour's given,
  In Jesus' name, the glorious theme, we elevate our voices,
  At Jesus' birth be peace on earth, meanwhile all heaven rejoices.

7 Then with delight they took their flight, and wing'd their way to glory,
  The shepherds gazed and were amazed, to hear the pleasing story;
  To Bethlehem they quickly came, the glorious news to carry,
  And in the stall they found them all, Joseph, the Babe, and Mary.

8 The shepherds then return'd again to their own habitation,
  With joy of heart they did depart, now they have found salvation.
  Glory, they cry, to God on high, who sent his Son to save us.
  This glorious morn the Saviour's born, his name is Christ Jesus.

56 TONE THE BELL EASY

1 When you hear dat I's a-dyin',
  I don' want nobody to mo'n.
  All I want my frien's to do
  Is give dat bell a tone.
    Well, well, well, tone de bell easy,
    Well, well, well, tone de bell easy,
    Well, well, well, tone de bell easy,
    Jesus gonna make up my dyin' bed.

2 Mary was a-grievin';
  Martha said: He isn' los',
  But late dat Friday evenin'
  He was hangin' to de cross.
    Well, well, well, he was hangin' in mis'ry, etc.

3 Jesus said to his disciples:
  I can see you are afraid;
  But if you keep my commandments,
  I'm gonna make up yo' dyin' bed.
    Well, well, well, he's my dyin'-bed maker, etc.

4 When you see me dyin',
  I don't want you to make no alarms;
  For I can see King Jesus comin'
  To fol' my dyin' arms.
      Well, well, well, he's my soul's 'mancipator, etc.

5 When you hear dat I'm a-dyin',
  I don't want you to be afraid;
  All I want my frièn's to do
  Is take de pillow from under my head.
      Well, well, well, so I can die easy, etc.

6 Mother on her dyin' bed,
  Children roun' her bed, cryin'.
  Go 'way, children, don' worry my min',
  'Cause you know I's born to die.
      Well, well, well, I don' min' dyin', etc.

7 When I had a mother,
  I had somewhere to go;
  But since my mother's been dead and gone,
  I been wand'rin' frum do' to do'.
      Well, well, well, I got good religion, etc.

8 Ever since me an' Jesus been married
  We haven' been a minute apart;
  He put the receiver in my han'
  An' de Holy Ghos' in my heart.
      Well, well, well, so I kin call up Jesus, etc.

9 Oh, meet me, Jesus, meet me,
  Meet me in de middle o' de air,
  So's if my wings should fail me,
  Please meet me wid another pair.
      Well, well, well, so I kin fly to Jesus, etc.

10 When you hear I'm dyin'
   Some one'll say I'm los';
   But jes' come down to de Jerdon
   An' ask de ferryman did I cross.
       Well, well, well, I'll be done cross over, etc.

11 When you hear I'm dyin',
   I don' want you to mo'n;
   All I want my frien's to do
   Is give dat bell a tone.
       Well, well, well, tone de bell easy,
       Well, well, well, tone de bell easy,
       Well, well, well, tone de bell easy,
       Jesus gonna make up my dyin' bed.

57 GIDEON'S BAND

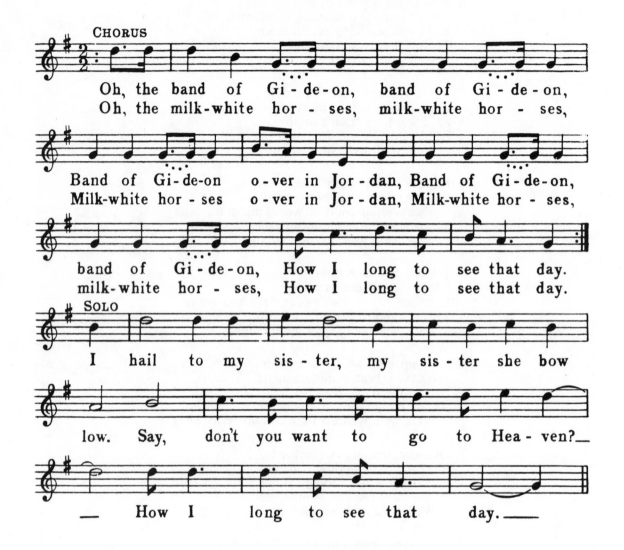

Chorus
Oh, the band of Gideon, band of Gideon,
Band of Gideon over in Jordan,
Band of Gideon, band of Gideon,
How I long to see that day.
Oh, the milk-white horses, milk-white horses,
Milk-white horses over in Jordan,
Milk-white horses, milk-white horses,
How I long to see that day.

1 I hail to my sister, my sister she bow low.
  Say, don't you want to go to Heaven?
  How I long to see that day.

> *Chorus*
> Oh, ride up in the chariot, ride up in the chariot,
> Ride up in the chariot over in Jordan,
> Ride up in the chariot, ride up in the chariot,
> How I long to see that day.
> It's a golden chariot, a golden chariot,
> Golden chariot over in Jordan,
> Golden chariot, a golden chariot,
> How I long to see that day.

2 I hail to my brother, my brother he bow low,
  Say, don't you want to go to Heaven?
  How I long to see that day.

> *Chorus*
> Oh, the milk and honey, milk and honey,
> Milk and honey over in Jordan,
> Milk and honey, milk and honey,
> How I long to see that day.
> Oh, the healing water, healing water,
> Healing water over in Jordan,
> Healing water, the healing water,
> How I long to see that day.

58 LAY DIS BODY DOWN

O grave-yard, O grave-yard, I'm walk-in' through de grave-yard; Lay dis bo-dy down.

1 O graveyard,
   O graveyard,
   I'm walkin' through de graveyard;
   Lay dis body down.

2 I know moonlight,
   I know starlight,
   I'm walkin' through de starlight;
   Lay dis body down.

3 I lay in de grave
   An' stretch out my arms,
   I'm layin' in de graveyard;
   Lay dis body down.

59 I'LL HEAR THE TRUMPET SOUND

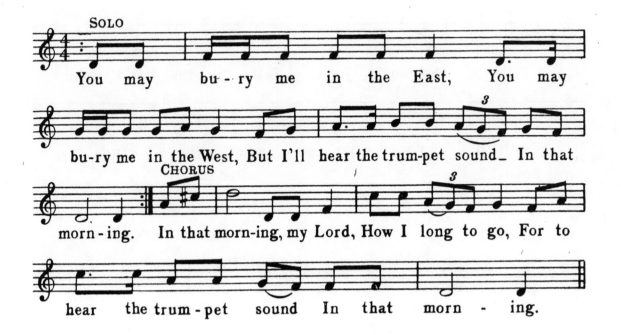

1 You may bury me in the East,
  You may bury me in the West,
  But I'll hear the trumpet sound
  In that morning.

   Chorus
   In that morning, my Lord,
   How I long to go,
   For to hear the trumpet sound
   In that morning.

2 Father Gabriel in that day,
  He'll take wings and fly away,
  For to hear the trumpet sound
  In that morning.

3 Good old Christians in that day,
  They'll take wings and fly away,
  For to hear the trumpet sound
  In that morning.

4 Good old preachers in that day,
  They'll take wings and fly away,
  For to hear the trumpet sound
  In that morning.

5 In that dreadful Judgment day,
  I'll take wings and fly away,
  For to hear the trumpet sound
  In that morning.

   Chorus
   In that morning, my Lord,
   How I long to go,
   For to hear the trumpet sound
   In that morning.

60 TELL ALL THE WORLD, JOHN

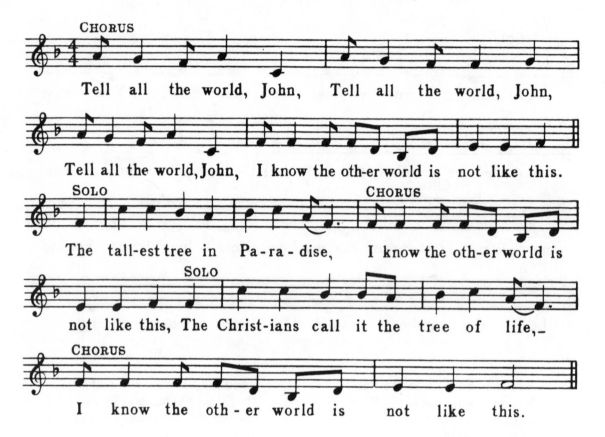

Chorus
Tell all the world, John,
Tell all the world, John,
Tell all the world, John,
I know the other world is not like this.

1 The tallest tree in Paradise,
   I know the other world is not like this,
The Christians call it the tree of life,
   I know the other world is not like this.

Chorus
Tell all the world, John,
Tell all the world, John,
Tell all the world, John,
I know the other world is not like this.

2 Well, if religion was a thing that money
                     could buy,
   The rich would live and the poor would
                     die.

3 Well, I've never been to heaven, but I've
                     been told
   The gates are pearl and the streets are
                     gold.

4 One of these mornings bright and fair,
   I know the other world is not like this,
I'm going to meet my Saviour there,
   I know the other world is not like this.

Chorus
Tell all the world, John,
Tell all the world, John,
Tell all the world, John,
I know the other world is not like this.

61 PUT JOHN ON THE ISLAN'

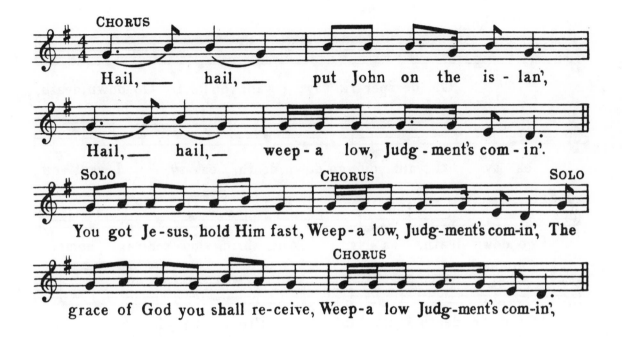

Hail, — hail, — put John on the is-lan',

Hail, — hail, — weep-a low, Judg-ment's com-in'.

SOLO You got Je-sus, hold Him fast, CHORUS Weep-a low, Judg-ment's com-in', SOLO The

grace of God you shall re-ceive, CHORUS Weep-a low Judg-ment's com-in',

Chorus
Hail, hail, put John on the islan',
Hail, hail, weep-a low, Judgment's comin'.

1 You got Jesus, hold Him fast,
   Weep-a low, Judgment's comin',
The grace of God you shall receive,
   Weep-a low, Judgment's comin'.

2 Didn't know Christ was into the field,
   Till I heard the rumblin' of the chariot wheel.

3 Goin' down Jordan to pay my fare,
   Have a little meetin' when I gits there.

4 Goin' up to Heaven, don't want to stop,
   Weep-a low, Judgment's comin',
Don't want to be no stumblin' block,
   Weep-a low, Judgment's comin'.

Chorus
Hail, hail, put John on the islan',
Hail, hail, weep-a low, Judgment's comin'.

62 GO DOWN, DEATH

1 Oh, de sperrit say: I want you for to
Go down, death, easy,
I want you go down, death, easy,
I want you go down, death, easy,
An' bring my servant home.

Chorus
Go down, death, go down.
Preach my glory an' my mighty name.
I want you go down, I want you go down,
An' bring my servant home.

2 Oh, de sperrit say: I want you for to
  Creep to de bedside easy,
  I want you creep to de bedside easy,
  I want you creep to de bedside easy,
  An' bring my servant home.

3 Oh, de sperrit say: I want you for to
  Close de eyelids easy,
  I want you close de eyelids easy,
  I want you close de eyelids easy,
  An' bring my servant home.

4 Oh, de sperrit say: I want you for to
  Cut loose de heart-strings easy,
  I want you cut loose de heart-strings easy,
  I want you cut loose de heart-strings easy,
  An' bring my servant home.

5 Oh, de sperrit say: I want you for to
  Step to de graveyard easy,
  I want you step to de graveyard easy,
  I want you step to de graveyard easy,
  An' bring my servant home.

6 Oh, de sperrit say: I want you for to
  Pass over hell-flames easy,
  I want you pass over hell-flames easy,
  I want you pass over hell-flames easy,
  An' bring my servant home.

7 Oh, de sperrit say: I want you for to
  March up in de Kingdom easy,
  I want you march up in de Kingdom easy,
  I want you march up in de Kingdom easy,
  An' bring my servant home.

    Chorus
    Go down, death, go down.
    Preach my glory an' my mighty name.
    I want you go down, I want you go down,
    An' bring my servant home.

63 DRY BONES

Down in de val-ley de sper-rit spoke: 'Ze-kul, go pro-phe-sy._

_ An' 'Ze-kul saw de val-ley full o' dead man's bones, An'

ev-er-y bone was dry. Dry bones gwine-a

gath-er in de morn-in', Come to-geth-er an' rise an'

shine._ Dry bones gwine-a gath-er in de val-ley, An'

some o' dem bones is mine.

1 Down in de valley de sperrit spoke:
'Zekul, go prophesy.
An' 'Zekul saw de valley full o' dead man's bones,
An' every bone was dry.

Chorus
Dry bones gwinea gather in de mornin',
Come together an' rise an' shine.
Dry bones gwinea gather in de valley,
An' some o' dem bones is mine.

2 Sperrit told 'Zekul call de four winds forth
An' breathe on de bones all slain.
Behold, he heard a noise, every bone to his bone
Come together an' lived again.

3 De graves all opened an' de bones took breath,
An' de skin covered over again,
And dey stood on dey feet like de army o' my Lawd,
Oh, de bones was livin' men!

Chorus
Some of dem bones is my mother's bones,
Come together for to rise an' shine.
Some o' dem bones is my father's bones,
An' some o' dem bones is mine.

Some o' dem bones gwinea make me laugh,
Come together for to rise an' shine.
Some o' dem bones gwinea make me weep,
'Cause some o' dem bones is mine.

MEXICO

64 SEÑORA SANTA ANA

(Lullaby)

Se - ño - ra San - ta A - na, ¿Por qué llo - ra el
ni - ño? Por u - na man - za - na Que se le ha per -
di - do. Duér - ma - se, ni - ño, Duér - ma - se
ya, Que ahí vie - ne el vie - jo Y se lo lle - va - rá.

1 Señora Santa Ana,
  ¿Por qué llora el niño?
  Por una manzana
  Que se le ha perdido. } (2)

1 Señora Sant' Ana,
  Why does baby cry?
  Oh, it's for an apple
  That he cannot find.

Refrain
Duérmase, niño,
Duérmase ya,
Que ahí viene el viejo
Y se lo llevará.

Hushabye, baby,
Sleep now, I pray,
Here comes an old man
To take you away.

2 Vamos a la huerta,
Cortaremos dos.
Una para el niño,
Y otra para vos. } (2)

3 Duérmase, niño,
Duérmase ya,
Que ahí viene el viejo
Y se lo llevará. } (2)

Refrain
Duérmase, niño,
Duérmase ya,
Que ahí viene el viejo
Y se lo llevará.

2 We'll go to the garden.
There we'll gather two.
One is for the baby,
The other is for you.

3 Close your eyes, my baby,
There now, do not weep.
Soon will come the sandman
To put you to sleep.

Hushabye, baby,
Sleep now, I pray.
Here comes an old man
To take you away.

V. K. and A. L. L.

65 MIREN CUÁNTAS LUCES

See how bright the heavens

(Caminata)

Mi - ren cuán - tas lu - ces, Cuán - tos res - plan -

do - res. Sin du - da es Be - lén.___ ¡Qué

glo - ria, pas - to - res! ¡Qué glo - ria, pas - to - res!

1 Miren cuántas luces,
   Cuántos resplandores.
   Sin duda es Belén.
   ¡Qué gloria, pastores! (2)

1 See how bright the heavens
   Are filled now with splendour!
   There lies Bethlehem.
   What glory, my shepherds! (2)

2 Aguas cristalinas
   Cómo estan vertiendo
   De las altas peñas
   Que vamos subiendo. (2)

2 And the crystal waters,
   How clear they are flowing
   From the highest hill-tops
   Where we are now going. (2)

3 Andale, Batito,
   Chíflale al ganado,
   Vamos a dar agua
   Al Río Colorado. (2)

3 Go along, Batito,
   And round up the wethers.
   We will give them water
   At Colorado River. (2)

4 ¡Qué cerros tan altos!
   Parece que ya
   Llegamos faciles
   Y sin novedad. (2)

4 How steep are the mountains,
   And hard for a stranger!
   Yet we climb them swiftly
   Without fear or danger. (2)

MEXICO

5 ¡Qué cerros tan altos!
　Lindos nos parece;
　Junten el ganado
　Porque ya amanece. (2)

6 Camina, Gilita,
　Que vendrás cansada;
　Por aquellos montes
　Haremos posada. (2)

7 Qué bonitas flores
　Hay por este cerro.
　Córtalas, Gilita,
　Para tu sombrero. (2)

8 ¡Albricias, pastores!
　Ya el gallo cantó.
　Clarito nos dice:
　¡Ya Cristo nació!

9 Areen la mulita,
　Bájenle el huacal,
　Saquen los tamales
　Para calentar. (2)

5 Lovely are these mountains,
　Skyward they are soaring.
　Let the sheep be gathered
　For daylight is dawning. (2)

6 Come along, Gilita,
　And don't you be weary;
　For among these mountains
　Our camp we are nearing. (2)

7 Lovely are the flowers
　In this valley fair, O.
　Pick a few, Gilita,
　To deck your sombrero. (2)

8 Dawn is coming, shepherds.
　The cock now is calling,
　And he tells us clearly
　That Christ is born this morning. (2)

9 Let us halt our donkey
　And take down the paniers,
　Then set out tamales
　To heat in the ashes. (2)

V. K.

66 EL CURA NO VA A LA IGLESIA

The curate won't go to church

(Tonadilla)

El cu-ra no va a la i-gle-sia. La ni-ña di-rá por

qué. Por-que no tie-ne za-pa-tos. Za-pa-tos yo le da-ré.

Los za-pa-tos con ta-cón, Ky-rie e-lei-són, Ky-rie e-lei-

són. El cu-ra no va a la i-gle-sia, La ni-ña di-rá por

qué. Por-que no tie-ne som-bre-ro. Som-bre-ro yo le da-ré.

El som-bre-ro es de ba-le-ro, La so-ta-na es de
El cha-le-co con su fle-co, La ca-mi-sa ya es-tá

la-na, La cha-que-ta de va-que-ta,   Las cal-ce-tas con so-
li-sta, Los cal-zo-nes con bo-to-nes,

le-tas, Los za-pa-tos con ta-cón, Ky-rie e-lei-són, Ky-rie e-lei-són.

1 El cura no va a la iglesia.
La niña dirá por qué.
Porque no tiene zapatos.
Zapatos yo le daré.
    Los zapatos con tacón.
    Kyrie eleisón.

2 El cura no va a la iglesia.
La niña dirá por qué.
Porque no tiene calcetas.
Calcetas yo le daré.
    Las calcetas con soletas,
    Los zapatos con tacón.
    Kyrie eleisón.

3 El cura no va a la iglesia.
La niña dirá por qué.
Porque no tiene calzones.
Calzones yo le daré.
    Los calzones con botones,
    Las calcetas con soletas,
    Los zapatos con tacón.
    Kyrie eleisón.

4 El cura no va a la iglesia.
La niña dirá por qué.
Porque no tiene camisa.
Camisa yo le daré.
    La camisa ya está lista,
    Los calzones con botones,
    Las calcetas con soletas,
    Los zapatos con tacón.
    Kyrie eleisón.

5 El cura no va a la iglesia.
La niña dirá por qué.
Porque no tiene chaleco.
Chaleco yo le daré.
    El chaleco con su fleco,
    La camisa ya está lista,
    Los calzones con botones,
    Las calcetas con soletas,
    Los zapatos con tacón.
    Kyrie eleisón.

6 El cura no va a la iglesia.
La niña dirá por qué.
Porque no tiene chaqueta.
Chaqueta yo le daré.
    La chaqueta de vaqueta,
    El chaleco con su fleco,
    La camisa ya está lista,
    Los calzones con botones,
    Las calcetas con soletas,
    Los zapatos con tacón.
    Kyrie eleisón.

1 The curate won't go to church, ma'am,
And Lisa can tell you why:
Because he has got no slippers,
So slippers I'll have to buy,
    Oh, some slippers to put on,
    Kyrie eleison.

2 The curate won't go to church, ma'am,
And Lisa can tell you why:
Because he has got no socks; and
So socks I will have to buy.
    Silken socks with gaudy clocks, and
    Oh, some slippers to put on,
    Kyrie eleison.

3 The curate won't go to church, ma'am,
And Lisa can tell you why:
Because he has got no breeches,
So breeches I'll have to buy.
    Little breeches, fancy stitches,
    Silken socks with gaudy clocks, and
    Oh, some slippers to put on,
    Kyrie eleison.

4 The curate won't go to church, ma'am,
And Lisa can tell you why:
Because he has got no shirt, and
So shirt I will have to buy.
    Stripy shirt all streaked with dirt, and
    Little breeches, fancy stitches,
    Silken socks with gaudy clocks, and
    Oh, some slippers to put on,
    Kyrie eleison.

5 The curate won't go to church, ma'am,
And Lisa can tell you why:
Because he has got no vest, and
So vest I will have to buy.
    Woolly vest for his weak chest, and
    Stripy shirt all streaked with dirt, and
    Little breeches, fancy stitches,
    Silken socks with gaudy clocks, and
    Oh, some slippers to put on,
    Kyrie eleison.

6 The curate won't go to church, ma'am,
And Lisa can tell you why:
Because he has got no jacket,
So jacket I'll have to buy.
    Elegant coat that smells of goat, and
    Woolly vest for his weak chest, and
    Stripy shirt all streaked with dirt, and
    Little breeches, fancy stitches,
    Silken socks with gaudy clocks, and
    Oh, some slippers to put on,
    Kyrie eleison.

continued on next page

66 (concluded)

7 El cura no va a la iglesia.
La niña dirá por qué.
Porque no tiene sotana.
Sotana yo le daré.
   La sotana es de lana,
   La chaqueta de vaqueta,
   El chaleco con su fleco,
   La camisa ya está lista,
   Los calzones con botones,
   Las calcetas con soletas,
   Los zapatos con tacón.
   Kyrie eleisón.

7 The curate won't go to church, ma'am,
And Lisa can tell you why:
Because he has no soutane, and
So soutane I'll have to buy.
   Black soutane wide as a barn, and
   Elegant coat that smells of goat, and
   Woolly vest for his weak chest, and
   Stripy shirt all streaked with dirt, and
   Little breeches, fancy stitches,
   Silken socks with gaudy clocks, and
   Oh, some slippers to put on,
   Kyrie eleison.

8 El cura no va a la iglesia.
La niña dirá por qué.
Porque no tiene sombrero.
Sombrero yo le daré.
   El sombrero es de balero,
   La sotana es de lana,
   La chaqueta de vaqueta,
   El chaleco con su fleco,
   La camisa ya está lista,
   Los calzones con botones,
   Las calcetas con soletas,
   Los zapatos con tacón.
   Kyrie eleisón.

8 The curate won't go to church, ma'am,
And Lisa can tell you why:
Because he has got no hat, and
So hat I will have to buy.
   Shovel hat that's pancake flat, and
   Black soutane wide as a barn, and
   Elegant coat that smells of goat, and
   Woolly vest for his weak chest, and
   Stripy shirt all streaked with dirt, and
   Little breeches, fancy stitches,
   Silken socks with gaudy clocks, and
   Oh, some slippers to put on,
   Kyrie eleison.

A. L. L.

67 MALHAYA LA CONCINA

Oh, cursed be the kitchen fire

(Tonadilla)

¡Mal - ha - ya la co - ci - na, ____ Mal - ha - ya el hu - mo! _ Y la mu-jer que cree ____ En hom-bre al - gu - no. ____ Por - que son ta - les, ____ Por-que son ta - les, _ Por-que to-dos los hom-bres, ¡Ca - ram - ba! ____ son in - for - ma - les. ____

1 ¡Malhaya la cocina, Malhaya el humo! Y la mujer que cree En hombre alguno. Porque son tales, Porque son tales, Porque todos los hombres ¡Caramba! son informales.	1 Oh, cursed be the kitchen fire, Curst be the oven! The woman who'd believe in man Is just a sloven. And here's the reason, And here's the reason: Because, I tell you, men Ay, caramba! are rogues and villains.
2 Pasé por una fragua, Dije al herrero: – Hágame usted un hombre De fino acero. Él me responde, Él me responde: – ¿Cómo quiere sea firme ¡Caramba! si ha de ser hombre?	2 One day as by a forge I went, – O smith, I pleaded, Make me a man to please my bent. True steel is needed. And thus he answered, And thus he answered: Oh, how could it be true, Ay, caramba! if it's of mankind?
3 Iba yo en una barca Con una cesta. Mi madre me pregunta: – ¿Qué fruta es esta? Y yo le digo, Y yo le digo: – Son unas calabazas !Caramba! para un amigo.	3 To take a boat across the sea, From home I started. And my good mother said to me: What's in your basket? And thus I answered, And thus I answered: It's just two little pumpkins, Caramba! to please my sweetheart.

V. K. and A. L. L.

68 EL MATRIMONIO DESIGUAL

The Mismatched Couple

(Tonadilla)

-Vie - ji - to, va - mos a mi - sa, Que le a -
ca - ban de lla - mar. -No las quie - ro tan de -
vo - tas. Sién - te - se a - hí a re - men - dar.

1 -- Viejito, vamos a misa,
   Que le acaban de llamar.
 - No las quiero tan devotas.
 Siéntese ahí a remendar.

1 – Let us go to mass, old husband.
   Listen how they toll the bell.
 – There's no need for such devotions.
 Sit and mend and you'll do as well.

MEXICO

2 – ¡Qué bonita está la plaza!
  Viejito, ¿me dejas ir?
  – Esté fea o esté bonita,
  Tú a la plaza no me has de ir.

3 – ¡Qué lindos están los toros!
  Viejito, ¿me dejas ir?
  – Estén lindos o estén *feyos,*
  Tú a los toros no me has de ir.

4 – ¡Válgame Dios de los cielos!
  ¿Qué haré yo con este viejo?
  – Me ha de amar, me ha de querer,
  Y me ha de ver como un espejo.

2 – Oh, how lovely is the plaza!
  Old man, will you let me go?
  – Be it beautiful or ugly,
  I will always answer 'No'.

3 – How exciting are the bull-fights!
  Old man, will you let me go?
  – Be they fine or be they wretched,
  I will always answer 'No'.

4 –Rescue me, O God in heaven!
  What to do with this old man?
  – You must always do as I do,
  And love me as best you can!

V. K.

69 LAS OLAS DE LA LAGUNA

The waves upon the lagoon

(Son)

¡Ay ay ay ay ay! Las o - las de la la - gu - na, —

— ¡Ay ay ay ay ay! U - nas vie - nen y o - tras van. —

— ¡Ay ay ay ay ay! U - nas van pa - ra Sa - yu - la, —

— ¡Ay ay ay ay ay! — Y o - tras pa - ra Za - po - tlán. —

1   ¡Ay ay ay ay ay!
Las olas de la laguna,
  ¡Ay ay ay ay ay!
Unas vienen y otras van.
  ¡Ay ay ay ay ay!
Unas van para Sayula,
  ¡Ay ay ay ay ay!
Y otras para Zapotlán.

1   Ay ay ay ay ay!
The waves upon the lagoon, love,
  Ay ay ay ay ay!
Some are coming, others gone.
  Ay ay ay ay ay!
Some are flowing to Sayula,
  Ay ay ay ay ay!
Others flow to Zapotlan.

2   ¡Ay ay ay ay ay!
    Allá va mi corazón
       ¡Ay ay ay ay ay!
    Sobre una viga nadando.
       ¡Ay ay ay ay ay!
    Que dice ese amor *engrido*
       ¡Ay ay ay ay ay!
    Con el que me estás pagando?

3   ¡Ay ay ay ay ay!
    Indita, vamos al mar
       ¡Ay ay ay ay ay!
    Y ahí nos embarcaremos.
       ¡Ay ay ay ay ay!
    Tu cuerpo será el navío,
       ¡Ay ay ay ay ay!
    Tus brazos serán los remos.

4   ¡Ay ay ay ay ay!
    Indita, vamos al mar.
       ¡Ay ay ay ay ay!
    Verás la mar y sus olas,
       ¡Ay ay ay ay ay!
    Verás a los marineros
       ¡Ay ay ay ay ay!
    Con banderas españolas.

2   Ay ay ay ay ay!
    There goes my poor broken heart, love,
       Ay ay ay ay ay!
    All adrift upon a beam.
       Ay ay ay ay ay!
    Why are you so proud and haughty?
       Ay ay ay ay ay!
    Why do you so mock my dreams?

3   Ay ay ay ay ay!
    Let us go down to the sea, love,
       Ay ay ay ay ay!
    And we'll take off from these shores.
       Ay ay ay ay ay!
    Your fair body is my ship, love,
       Ay ay ay ay ay!
    And your arms shall be the oars.

4   Ay ay ay ay ay!
    Let us go down to the sea, love,
       Ay ay ay ay ay!
    And survey the rolling main,
       Ay ay ay ay ay!
    Where the sailors sing so free, love,
       Ay ay ay ay ay!
    Mid the fluttering flags of Spain.

                        V. K. and A. L. L.

70 CAJEME

(Corrido)

¡Qué bo - ni - to Río de Ma - yo!_ ¡Qué bo - ni - to Río de Ma - yo!_ Mé - tan - se, que no es - tá jon - do._ Les trae - re-mos un guay - me - ño, Les trae - re-mos un guay - me - ño Que les dé vuel-ta en re - don - do._

1 ¡Qué bonito Río de Mayo! (2)
   Métanse, que no está jondo.
   Les traeremos un guaymeño (2)
   Que les dé vuelta en redondo.

2 Ese don Lorenzo Torres (2)
   Es un hombre muy cobarde.
   Para entregar a Cajeme, (2)
   Primero lo hizo compadre.

3 Dicen que Cajeme ha muerto.
   No es verdá, no ha muerto nada.
   Anda con todos sus indios (2)
   Para la Sierra Mojada.

4 Si se quieren divertir (2)
   Bájense para El Añil,
   Que allí estoy con mis inditos (2)
   Poco más de cuatro mil.

1 Oh, that lovely Mayo river! (2)
   Wade across the shallow water
   And we'll take 'em by surprise, boys, (2)
   And we won't give any quarter.

2 Oh, that don Lorenzo Torres, (2)
   He's a craven-hearted hombre,
   And to catch our bold Cajeme, (2)
   He made out to be his comrade.

3 Now they say Cajeme's dead, boys. (2)
   It's a lie, for he's still riding,
   And he's off with all his Indians (2)
   'cross the wild Sierra Mojada.

4 If you're looking for amusement, (2)
   Take a trip into our mountains,
   For I'm here with all my Indians, (2)
   And we're just about four thousand.

A. L. L.

GUATEMALA

71 NACÍ EN LA CUMBRE

I was born on the mountain

1 Nací en la cumbre de una montaña
   Librando el rayo desbastador;
   Crecí en el fondo de una cabaña,
   Y hoy que soy hombre muero de amor.

1 Well, I was born, love, born on the
                              mountain,
   Rocks all around me and the sun above;
   Grew up in back of a little cabin;
   Now I'm a grown man, I die for love.

2 Unos bandidos me alimentaron,
   A la cuitada que me dió el ser;
   Hijo del Trueno me apellidaron,
   Y en noche obscura vine a nacer.

2 A band of outlaws they came and fed me,
   And the poor woman who gave me birth.
   Son of the Thunder was what they called
                              me;
   And since that dark night I am accurst.

3 Si tú no sales a tu ventana,
   Perla de Oriente, nítida flor,
   Cabe tus muros verás manana
   Rota mi lira, muerto al cantor.

3 Sweet flower, open your bedroom
                              window.
   Star of the Orient, rise from your bed,
   Or you will find, love, soon in the
                              morning,
   My guitar broken, the singer dead.

A. L. L.

72 VAMOS A LA MAR

Let's go to the sea

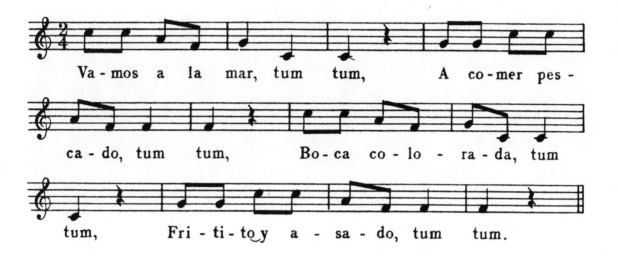

Va - mos a la mar, tum tum, A co - mer pes -
ca - do, tum tum, Bo - ca co - lo - ra - da, tum
tum, Fri - ti - to y a - sa - do, tum tum.

1 Vamos a la mar, tum tum,
A comer pescado, tum tum,
Boca colorada, tum tum,
Fritito y asado, tum tum.

2 Vamos a la mar, tum tum,
A comer pescado, tum tum,
Fritito y asado, tum tum,
En sartén de palo, tum tum.

1 Let's go to the sea, tum tum,
Hook some fish and try 'em, tum tum.
Mouth as red as ruby, tum tum,
Barbecue or fry 'em.

2 Let's go to the sea, tum tum,
Catch a fish and grill it, tum tum,
Barbecue or fry it, tum tum,
In a wooden skillet, tum tum.

A. L. L.

HONDURAS

73 FLORES DE MIMÉ

Mimé Flowers

1 A la orilla del Río Verbena
   De Maromé, flores de mimé,
Tengo sembrado
Azafrán y canela, verbena
   De Maromé, flores de mimé,
Pimienta y clavo.

1 By the side of the Rio Verbena
   In Maromé, where flowers do grow,
There I have planted
Sweetest cinnamon, saffron, verbena
   In Maromé, where flowers do grow,
And cloves and peppers.

HONDURAS

2 En la falda de la montaña
   De Maromé, flores de mimé,
Están sembrando
Un yucal, un canal y canela
   De Maromé, flores de mimé,
Y maíz morado.

3 Quando quiero cantarle a mi chata
   De Maromé, flores de mimé,
Con mi guitarra,
Ensillo mi caballo plateado,
   De Maromé, flores de mimé,
Y voy montado.

4 A la orilla del Río Verbena
   De Maromé, flores de mimé,
Tengo sembrado
Azafrán y canela, verbena
   De Maromé, flores de mimé,
Pimienta y clavo.

2 On the slope of the gentle mountain
   In Maromé, where flowers do grow,
There they are planting
Sugar-cane, cinnamon and white yuccas,
   In Maromé, where flowers do grow,
Red maize and barley.

3 When I want to sing to my dear
                    sweetheart
   In Maromé, where flowers do grow,
With my guitar, boys,
Well, I saddle my silver-grey pony,
   In Maromé, where flowers do grow,
And go a-riding.

4 By the side of the Rio Verbena
   In Maromé, where flowers do grow,
There I have planted
Sweetest cinnamon, saffron, verbena
   In Maromé, where flowers do grow,
And cloves and peppers.

A. L. L.

74 EL SAPO

The Frog

Guitar

sa-po es un a - ni mal Que no tie - ne buen ta -

lan-te, Chi-mi-chi-mi - ni-que, chi-mi-chi-mi - ni - que,

¡Que no tie-ne buen ta - lan-te, eh!_____ Pe -

ro en su con - ver - sa - ción Pue-de ser un co-man-

dan-te, Chi-mi-chi-mi - ni-que, chi-mi-chi-mi - ni - que,

Fin ¡Pue-de ser un co-man-dan - te, eh!_____

El sa po es un a - ni - mal,

124

HONDURAS

Chi - mi - chi - mi - chi - mi - ni - que, El sa - po es un a - ni -

mal, Chi - mi - chi - mi - chi - mi - ni - que. ___

1 El sapo es un animal
  Que no tiene buen talante,
  Chimi-chiminique, chimi-chiminique,
  ¡Que no tiene buen talante, eh!
  Pero en su conversación
  Puede ser un comandante,
  Chimi-chiminique, chimi-chiminique,
  ¡Puede ser un comandante, eh!

2 Cuando está en sociedad,
  Siempre su presencia grata,
  Chimi-chiminique, chimi-chiminique,
  ¡Siempre su presencia grata, eh!
  Haciendo genuflexiones
  Y hablando pura lata,
  Chimi-chiminique, chimi-chiminique,
  ¡Y hablando pura lata, eh!

3 En el amor es experto,
  Y en eso tiene el secreto,
  Chimi-chiminique, chimi-chiminique,
  ¡Y en eso tiene el secreto, oh!
  Enemigo del trabajo,
  Muy bailador y discreto,
  Chimi-chiminique, chimi-chiminique,
  ¡Muy bailador y discreto, oh!

4 El sapo es un animal,
  Chimi-chimi-chiminique,
  El sapo es un animal,
  Chimi-chimi-chiminique.

1 The frog is an animal,
  Nothing special in his favour,
  Chimi-chiminique, chimi-chiminique,
  Nothing special in his favour, eh!
  But simply to hear him talk,
  You'd think he's at least a major,
  Chimi-chiminique, chimi-chiminique,
  You'd think he's at least a major, eh!

2 When he's in society,
  Well, he's always full of flourish,
  Chimi-chiminique, chimi-chiminique,
  Well, he's always full of flourish, eh!
  Yes, making his little bows,
  Talking such a load of rubbish,
  Chimi-chiminique, chimi-chiminique,
  Talking such a load of rubbish, eh!

3 In love he's a real expert,
  To such things he knows the answer,
  Chimi-chiminique, chimi-chiminique,
  To such things he knows the answer, oh!
  He hates any kind of work,
  Fancies himself as a dancer,
  Chimi-chiminique, chimi-chiminique,
  Fancies himself as a dancer, oh!

4 The frog is an animal,
  Chimi-chimi-chiminique,
  The frog is an animal,
  Chimi-chimi-chiminique.

A. L. L.

75 PAPANULAN

Pa-pa-nu-lan, Pa-pa-nu-lan, Tra-ba-

jan-do el dí - a no - che,___ ¡Ay! Pa-pa-

nu - lan, Pa-pa-nu-lan, vi-da mí - a.___

Tra-ba-jan-do el dí - a no - che, Ga-

nan-cio cua-ren-ta pe - so, ¡Ay! Pa-pa-

nu - lan, Pa-pa-nu-lan, vi-da mí - a.___

1 Papanulan, Papanulan,
  Trabajando el día noche,
  ¡Ay! Papanulan,
  Papanulan, vida mía.

2 Trabajando el día noche,
  Ganancio cuarenta peso,
  ¡Ay! Papanulan,
  Papanulan, vida mía.

3 Trabajando el día noche,
  Ganancio cuarenta peso,
  ¡Ay! Papanulan,
  Trabajando el día noche.

4 Papanulan, Papanulan,
  Papanulan, vida mía,
  Quiero que si me astumba
  Me alegre tamburira.

1 Papanola, Papanola,
  Well, I'm working day and night here,
  Ay! Papanola,
  Papanola, my own darling.

2 Well, I'm working day and night here,
  I make only forty pesos.
  Ay! Papanola,
  Papanola, my own darling.

3 Oh, it's working day and night here,
  I make only forty pesos.
  Ay! Papanola,
  Yes, for working day and night here.

4 Papanola, Papanola,
  Papanola, my own darling,
  I want you, if you bury me
  To rattle the drum merrily.

A. L. L.

COSTA RICA

COSTA RICA

76 EL TORO PINTO

The spotted Bull

1 Echáme ese toro pinto,
   Hijo de la vaca mora,
   Para sacarle una suerte
   Delante de mi señora.
     ¡Que te coge el toro, Simona,
     Que te coge el toro, Marcela! } (2)

1 Go, loose me the spotted bull now,
   The son of the piebald heifer,
   That I may try a few passes
   To gain my dear sweetheart's favour.
     Mind, the bull will get you, Simona,
     Mind, the bull will get you, Marcela! } (2)

128

2 Si ese toro me matare,
No me entierren en sagrado.
Entierrenme en campo afuera,
Donde me pise el ganado.

3 No murió de calentura,
Ni de dolor al costado;
Murió de una cornada
Que le dió el toro pintado.

4 Allá en aquel rincón
Pintado de colorado,
Alli están las cinco letras
Donde murió el desdichado.
    ¡Que te coge el toro, Simona,
    Que te coge el toro, Marcela! } (2)

2 And if the young bull should kill me,
Just lay me down over yonder.
Don't bury me in the graveyard,
But where the wild cattle wander.

3 It wasn't the heat that killed him,
Nor pain, nor yet any fever;
The young spotted bull it gored him
And now he is lost for ever.

4 And over there in the corner
All spotted with crimson colour,
Just five letters mark the place where
They laid the unlucky lover.
    Mind, the bull will get you, Simona,
    Mind, the bull will get you, Marcela! } (2)

A. L. L.

129

77 ¡AY! TITUY

1 ¡Ay! ti - tuy, ___ ay! ti - tuy, ___ ¡Ay! ti - tuy, qui - ni -
nuy, qui - ni - nuy. ___ Ay! ti - tuy, ___ ¡ay ti - tuy, ___
___ ¡Ay! ti - tuy, qui - ni - nuy, qui - ni - nuy. ___ ¡Ay! ti -
tuy. ___ La pie - dra que mu - cho rue - da ___
No sir - ve pa - ra ci - mien - to, ___ Co - mo el
hom - bre ___ sin - ver - güen - za, ___ Que no tra - ta de
ca - sa - mien - to. ___ 2 Me sa - do. ___ ¡Ay! ti -

1 ¡Ay! tituy, ay! tituy,	1 Ay, tituy! Ay, tituy!
¡Ay! tituy, quininuy, quininuy.	Ay, tituy, quininuy, quininuy!
¡Ay! tituy, ay! tituy,	Ay, tituy! Ay, tituy!
¡Ay! tituy, quininuy, quininuy.	Ay, tituy, quininuy, quininuy!
La piedra que mucho rueda	The stone that is always rolling
No sirve para cimiento,	Is no good for a foundation,
Como el hombre sinvergüenza,	Nor the man who will not marry
Que no trata de casamiento.	But whose heart is set on flirtation.

2 Me dices que no me quieres,
  Porque no te ha dado nada.
  Acordate del centavo
  Que te dí el año pasado.
    ¡Ay! tituy, ay! tituy,
    ¡Ay! tituy, quininuy, quininuy.
    ¡Ay! tituy, ay! tituy,
    ¡Ay! tituy, quininuy, quininuy.

2 You say that I give you nothing,
  But there you're speaking too fast, dear.
  Just remember that centavo
  That I gave you, why, only last year.

3 Me dices que no me quieres,
  Porque yo te dí mal pago.
  Volveme a querer de nuevo,
  Porque un clavo saca otro clavo.
    ¡Ay! tituy, ay! tituy,
    ¡Ay! tituy, quininuy, quininuy.
    ¡Ay! tituy, ay! tituy,
    ¡Ay! tituy, quininuy, quininuy.

3 You say that you do not love me
  Because I cause too much bother.
  I suggest you come back to me
  Because one nail drives in another.
    Ay, tituy! Ay, tituy!
    Ay, tituy, quininuy, quininuy!
    Ay, tituy! Ay, tituy!
    Ay, tituy, quininuy, quininuy!

A. L. L.

PANAMA

78 HOJITA DE GUARUMAL

Green leaf of the guarumo

1 Hojita de guarumal, Don-de vi-ve la lan-gos-ta, Don-de co-me, don-de duer-me, Don-de vi-ve la lan-gos-ta. 2 Ho-gos-ta.

1 **Hojita de guarumal,**
   Donde vive la langosta,
   Donde come, donde duerme,
   Donde vive la langosta.

1 **Green leaf of the guarumo,**
   On it lives the little locust.
   There he eats and there he's sleeping;
   There he lives, the little locust.

2 **Hojita de guarumal,**
   Donde vive la langosta,
   Donde come, donde cena,
   Donde duerme la langosta.

2 **Green leaf of the guarumo,**
   On it lives the little locust.
   There he eats and there he's feasting;
   There he sleeps, the little locust.

3 **Hojita de guarumal,**
   Donde vive la langosta,
   Donde come, donde toma,
   Donde duerme la langosta.

3 **Green leaf of the guarumo,**
   On it lives the little locust.
   There he eats and there he's drinking;
   There he sleeps, the little locust.

4 **Hojita de guarumal,**
   Donde vive la langosta,
   Donde come, donde duerme,
   Donde muere la langosta.

4 **Green leaf of the guarumo,**
   On it lives the little locust.
   There he eats and there he's sleeping;
   There he'll die, the little locust.

A. L. L.

79 MI POLLERA

My skirt

1 Mi po - lle - ra, mi po - lle - ra, Mi po - lle - ra es co - lo - ra - da. Yo quie - ro u - na po - lle - ra de o - lán de co - co. Si tú no me las das, me voy con o - tro. 2 Mi po - ti - go.

1 Mi pollera, mi pollera,
Mi pollera es colorada.
Yo quiero una pollera de olán de coco.
Si tú no me las das, me voy con otro.

1 Oh, my frills and oh, my flounces,
I've a skirt that's red in colour.
I wish I had a skirt with those calico
flounces,
So buy me one or else I'll love another.

2 Mi pollera, mi pollera,
Mi pollera es colorada.
La tuya es blanca, la mía es rosada,
Mi pollera es colorada.

2 Oh, my frills and oh, my flounces,
I've a skirt of crimson colour,
And yours is snow-white, mine is rose
red,
Oh, my skirt of crimson colour!

3 Mi pollera, mi pollera,
Mi pollera es colorada.
Yo quiero una pollera de olán de hilo.
Si tú me la das, me voy contigo.

3 Oh, my frills and oh, my flounces,
I've a skirt that's red in colour.
I wish I had a skirt with those linen
flounces,
So buy me one and then I'll be your lover.

A. L. L.

BAHAMAS

80   DIG MY GRAVE LONG AN' NARROW

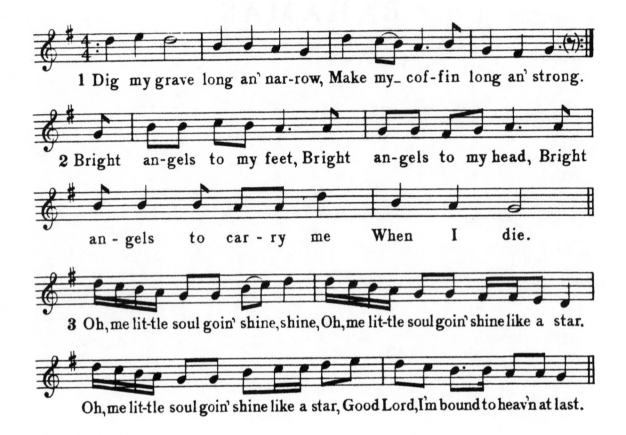

1 Dig my grave long an' nar-row, Make my_ cof-fin long an' strong.

2 Bright an-gels to my feet, Bright an-gels to my head, Bright

an - gels to car - ry me When I die.

3 Oh, me lit-tle soul goin' shine, shine, Oh, me lit-tle soul goin' shine like a star.

Oh, me lit-tle soul goin' shine like a star, Good Lord, I'm bound to heav'n at last.

1 Dig my grave long an' narrow,
  Make my coffin long an' strong. } (2)

2 Bright angels to my feet,
  Bright angels to my head,
  Bright angels to carry me
  When I die.

3 Oh, me little soul goin' shine, shine,
  Oh, me little soul goin' shine like a star.
  Oh, me little soul goin' shine like a star,
  Good Lord, I'm bound to heav'n at last.

BAHAMAS

81 THE WIND BLOW EAST

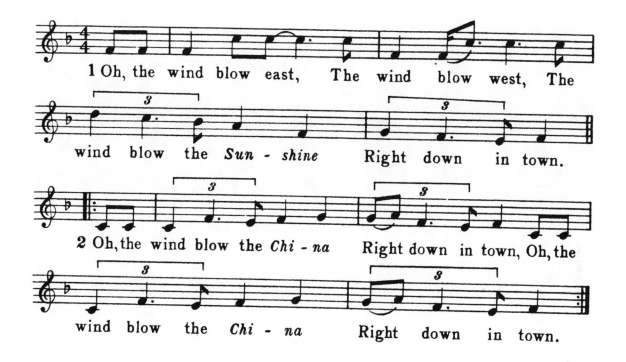

1 Oh, the wind blow east, The wind blow west, The wind blow the *Sun-shine* Right down in town.

2 Oh, the wind blow the *Chi-na* Right down in town, Oh, the wind blow the *Chi-na* Right down in town.

1 Oh, the wind blow east,
The wind blow west.
The wind blow the *Sunshine*
Right down in town.

2   Oh, the wind blow the *China* } (2)
Right down in town.

3 Oh, the wind blow east,
The wind blow west,
The wind blow the *Settin' Star*
Right down in town.

4   Oh, the wind blow the *Sunshine* } (2)
Right down in town.

(*The* Sunshine, China *and* Setting Star *are sloops, blown ashore by a hurricane.*)

139

CUBA

82 MÁ TEODORA
(Son)

Solo Chorus

–¿Don - de es - tá la Má Teo - do - ra? –Ra -

Solo Chorus

jan-do la le-ña es - tá.–¿Con su pa-lo y su ban-do-la? –Ra -

Solo Chorus

jan-do la le-ña es - tá.–¿Don-de es-tá que no la ve-o? –Ra -

jan-do la le-ña es - tá, Ra - jan-do la le-ña es - tá, Ra -

jan-do la le-ña es - tá, Ra - jan-do la le-ña es - tá.

CUBA

1 – ¿Donde está la Má Teodora?
– Rajando la leña está.
– ¿Con su palo y su bandola?
– Rajando la leña está.
– ¿Donde está que no la veo?
– Rajando la leña está,
Rajando la leña está,
Rajando la leña está,
Rajando la leña está.

1 – Where, O where is Ma Teodora?
– She's splitting up the fire-wood.
– With her stick and her bandola?
– She's splitting up the fire-wood.
– Where is she, for I don't see her?
– She's splitting up the fire-wood.
She's splitting up the fire-wood,
She's splitting up the fire-wood,
She's splitting up the fire-wood.

A. L. L.

Teodora Ginés, a freed Negress of Santiago de Cuba, was famous as a singer and dancer in the 16th century. 'Palo' (stick) probably refers to the staff she carried as dance-leader. 'Rajando la leña' (splitting wood) here means dancing (cf. 'cutting a rug').

83 YO QUISIERA VIVIR EN LA HABANA

(Habanera antigua)

Yo qui-sie-ra vi-vir en la Ha-ba-na, A pe-
sar, a pe-sar del ca-lor que ha-ce a-llí, Pa-sar la vi-da en
u-na ha-ma-ca, Pen-san-do en tí, Pen-san-do en ti. Yo no
pue-do vi-vir sin tí. A la Ha-ba-na he de vol-
ver En bus-ca de a-quel a-mor Que le da-bas a o-tra mu-
jer. 2 En la Ha-ba-na me re-ga-la-ron Un ta-
rri-to de ri-ca miel, Y al pro-bar-lo se des-per-
tó__ En mi pe-chi-to un nue-vo que-rer. Yo no

CUBA

pue-do vi-vir sin tí.   A la Ha-ba-na he de vol-ver   En

bus-ca de a-quel a-mor   Que le da-bas a o-tra mu-jer.

1 Yo quisiera vivir en la Habana,
   A pesar, a pesar del calor que hace allí,
   Pasar la vida en una hamaca,
   Pensando en tí, pensando en tí.
      Yo no puedo vivir sin tí.
      A la Habana he de volver
      En busca de aquel amor
      Que le dabas a otra mujer.

2 En la Habana me regalaron
   Un tarrito de rica miel,
   Y al probarlo se despertó
   En mi pechito un nuevo querer.
      Yo no puedo vivir sin tí.
      A la Habana he de volver
      En busca de aquel amor
      Que le dabas a otra mujer.

1 Oh, I wish that I lived in Havana,
   On account, on account of the heat in
                       this place,
   To pass the time in a silken hammock
   Just dreaming of your handsome face.
      For I can't live without my dear.
      To Havana I'll return
      To see if I find that love
      That you gave to some other girl.

2 And when I came to old Havana,
   Someone gave me a honeycomb,
   And the minute I tasted its sweetness,
   In my poor heart a new love had grown.
      For I can't live without my dear.
      To Havana I'll return
      To see if I find that love
      That you gave to some other girl.

A. L. L.

84 VAMOS A HACER UN AJIACO

We're going to make a fine stew

(Guaracha antigua)

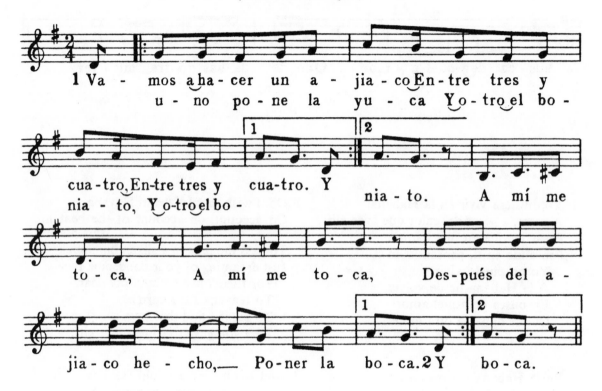

1 Va - mos a ha - cer un a - jia - co En - tre tres y
u - no po - ne la yu - ca Yo - tro el bo -

cua - tro, En-tre tres y cua-tro. Y
nia - to, Yo-tro el bo -

nia - to. A mí me

to - ca, A mí me to - ca, Des-pués del a -

jia - co he - cho,— Po-ner la bo - ca. 2 Y bo - ca.

1 Vamos a hacer un ajiaco
Entre tres y cuatro,
Entre tres y cuatro.
Y uno pone la yuca
Y otro el boniato,
Y otro el boniato.
  A mí me toca,
  A mí me toca,
  Después del ajiaco hecho,
  Poner la boca.
	1 We're going to make a fine stew, yes,
	Round about two, yes,
	Round about two, love.
	And in it we'll put some yucca,
	Some sweet potato,
	Likewise some rue, love.
	  It's all for me, girls.
	  Don't feel mistreated;
	  Soon as that *ajiaco*'s ready,
	  I'm going to eat it.

2 Y solo para el ajiaco
Se ha convidado,
Se ha convidado
La vecina de aquí en frente,
La de aquí al lado,
La de aquí al lado.
  A mí me toca,
  A mí me toca,
  Después del ajiaco hecho,
  Poner la boca.
	2 Now, on account of that stew
	It seems one or two folk
	Think they're invited.
	The neighbours over the way
	And some from the Bay
	Are looking delighted.
	  But it's for me, girls.
	  Don't feel mistreated;
	  Soon as that ajiaco's ready,
	  I'm going to eat it.

A. L. L.

85 AL AMANECER DEL DÍA

Just as day is dawning

(Tonada campesina)

Al a-ma-ne-cer del dí-a,   Por un flo-ri-do sen-de-ro,

Al a-ma-ne-cer del dí-a,   Por un flo-ri-do sen-de-ro,—

Trai-ra-rá,   So-bre mi po-tro jo-ve-ro,—   Trai-ra-rá,

Ga-llar-da i-rás, Lo-la mí-a,   Ga-llar-da i-rás, Lo-la mí-a.

1 Al amanecer del día,
  Por un florido sendero,
  Al amanecer del día,
  Por un florido sendero,
  Trairará,
  Sobre mi potro jovero,
  Trairará,
  Gallarda irás, Lola míra.
  Gallarda irás, Lola mía,

2 Y al llegar del medio día,
  Al pié de la fácil cuesta
  Que esta al fin de la floresta,
  Bajo las frondosas jaguas,
  Trairará,
  Al son de las frescas aguas,
  Trairará,
  Vendrás a pasar la siesta,
  Vendrás a pasar la siesta.

1 And it's just as day is dawning,
  All along the leafy pathway,
  And it's just as day is dawning,
  All along the leafy pathway,
  Trairará,
  On my little chestnut pony,
  Trairará,
  Lola rides out in the morning,
  Lola rides out in the morning.

2 And all in the blaze of noontide,
  At the foot of yonder mountain,
  Just beside the gentle fountain,
  In the shade of the green poplar,
  Trairará,
  Mid the sound of running water,
  Trairará,
  There she'll take her sweet siesta,
  There she'll take her sweet siesta.

A. L. L.

147

86 PARA LOS CAFICULTORES

For the coffee-workers

Pa-ra los ca-fi-cul-to-res Ya es-tá lle-gan-do el mi - nu - to,

Pa-ra los ca-fi-cul - to-res Ya es-tá   lle-gan-do el mi-nu-to,

De re-co-ger e-se fru-to,   Pro-duc-to de sus la-bo - res.

1 Para los caficultores
   Ya está llegando el minuto,
   Para los caficultores
   Ya está llegando el minuto,
   De recoger ese fruto,
   Producto de sus labores.

2 Ya en los primeros albores
   De agosto se empieza a ver
   El rojo grano caer
   Del frondoso cafetal,
   Y en un proceso inicial
   Lo empiezan a recoger.

1 Roll along, you coffee-workers,
   For your busy time is coming,
   Roll along, you coffee-workers,
   For your busy time is coming,
   And the plantations are humming
   Now the coffee's ripe for picking.

2 Soon in August we'll be seeing,
   In the first light of the morning,
   That the red berries are falling
   And the harvest has begun,
   Hear the coffee-workers calling
   As they toil from sun to sun.

A. L. L.

148

87 HAY AQUÍ, MADRE, UN JARDÍN

Mother, there's a garden fair

(Tonada campesina)

Hay a-quí, ma-dre, un jar-din No muy le-jos de mi es-tan-cía,

Hay a-quí, ma-dre, un jar-din No muy le-jos de mi es-

tan-cia, Pim pi-rim pim pi-rim pim pim pim, Don-de es-par-cen su fra-

gan-cia La dia-me-la y el jaz-mín. Es ver-dad.

1 Hay aquí, madre, un jardín
No muy lejos de mi estancia,
Hay aquí, madre, un jardín
No muy lejos de mi estancia,
Pim pirim pim pirim pim pim pim,
Donde esparcen su fragancia
La diamela y el jazmín.
Es verdad.

2 El zunzun y el tomeguín
Liban la blanca azucena,
Que en bella tarde serena
Mágico perfume exhala,
Pim pirim pim pirim pim pim pim,
Y crecen con toda gala
El clavel y la verbena.
Es verdad.

1 Mother, there's a garden fair
Not so far from my estancia,
Mother, there's a garden fair
Not so far from my estancia,
Pim pirim pim pirim pim pim pim,
Where the mignonette and jasmine
Spread their fragrance in the air.
It's the truth.

2 Humming bird and tomeguin
Suck the sweetness of the lily,
That gives off its perfume shyly
In the quiet of the evening,
Pim pirim pim pirim pim pim pim,
And carnation and verbena
Are found there in all their splendour.
It's the truth.

A. L. L.

HAITI

88 FOR ATTI DAÏ

(Cult Song)

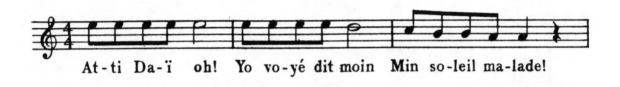

At-ti Da-ï oh! Yo vo-yé dit moin Min so-leil ma-lade!

Quan'm té ri-vé__ Moin joind so-leil mou-ri!__

Quan'm té ri-vé__ Moin joind so-leil mou-ri!

C'est re-gret-tant ça Pou'm en-ter-ré so-leil!

HAITI

1 Atti Daï oh!
  Yo voyé dit moin
  Min soleil malade!
  Quan'm té rivé
  Moin joind soleil mouri!
  Quan'm té rivé
  Moin joind soleil mouri!
  C'est regrettant ça
  Pou'm enterré soleil!

1 Atti Dai O,
  They sent to tell me
  That the sun was sick!
  And when I arrived
  I found the sun had died!
  And when I arrived,
  I found the sun had died!
  It's a grievous thing
  To bury the dead sun!

A. L. L.

Atti Dai is a Vodoun deity, also known as Attisole. Some believe that the word here given as "soleil" is in fact a diminutive form of the deity's other name.

89 JÉORICO

Angélique, Oh

Al - lé caille man-man ou,　　Al - lé caille man-man ou,

Al - lé caille man-man, ché-rie, ___ Pas vin' ba'm dé-sa-gré-ment!

Al - lé caille man-man, cher,　　Al - lé caille man-man, cher,

Al-lé caille man-man, mon cher, __ Pou' pas ba'm dé-sa-gré-ment!

Ti fille pas con' la-vé, pas-sé,　　Al-lé caille man-man ou!

Ti fille pas con'_ la-vé, __ pas-sé, ___ Al-lé caille man-man ou!

Jé - o - ri - co,　Jé - o - ri - co,　(mm) Al-lé caille man-man ou!

Jé - o - ri - co,　Jé - o - ri - co,　Al - lé caille man-man ou!

HAITI

1 Allé caille manman ou,
  Allé caille manman ou,
  Allé caille manman, chérie,
  Pas vin' ba'm désagrément!
  Allé caille manman, cher,
  Allé caille manman, cher,
  Allé caille manman, mon cher,
  Pou' pas ba'm désagrément!
  Ti fille pas con' lavé, passé,
  Allé caille manman ou!
  Ti fille pas con' lavé, passé,
  Allé caille manman ou!
  Jéorico, Jéorico,
  Allé caille manman ou!
  Jéorico, Jéorico,
  Allé caille manman ou!

1 Go to your mother's house,
  Go to your mother's house,
  Go back to her house, darling,
  Don't come and argue with me.
  Go back to mother, dear,
  Go back to mother, dear,
  Go back to mother, darling,
  So you don't argue with me.
  A girl who can't wash or iron,
  Go to your mother's house,
  A girl who can't wash or iron,
  Go to your mother's house.
  Angelique oh, Angélique oh,
  Go back to your mother dear,
  Angelique oh, Angélique oh,
  Go to your mother's house.

A. L. L.

JAMAICA

90 OH, SELINA

(Digging Song)

Oh,— Se - li - na!   Oh,— Se - li - na!

John Crow de a riv - er - side A call fe Se - li - na!

Oh, poor Se - li - na!   Dup - py an' all A

call fe Se - li - na! Oh, poor Se - li - na!

1 Oh, Selina!
   Oh, Selina!
John Crow de a riverside
A call fe Selina!
   Oh, poor Selina!
Duppy an' all
A call fe Selina!
   Oh, poor Selina!

Selina is drowned. By the riverside, the spirits of the dead are summoning her.

91 JOHN THOMAS

(Digging Song)

Oh! John Tho-mas, Oh! John Tho-mas, Oh! John Tho-mas Oh! John Tho-mas, We all a com-bo-low, John Tho-mas. Me go da 'le-ven mile, John Tho-mas, Me see one gal me love, John Tho-mas, Me court her all the way, John Tho-mas. Me come a Ban-ghe-son, John Tho-mas, Me buy one quat-tie bread, John Tho-mas, Me part it right in two, John Tho-mas, Me give her the big-gest piece, John Tho-mas, And-a war - ra more you want, John Tho-mas?

1 Oh! John Thomas,
   Oh! John Thomas,
Oh! John Thomas,
   Oh! John Thomas,
We all a combolow,
   John Thomas.
Me go da 'leven mile,
   John Thomas,
Me see one gal me love,
   John Thomas,
Me court her all the way,
   John Thomas.
Me come a Bangheson,
   John Thomas,
Me buy one quattie bread,
   John Thomas,
Me part it right in two,
   John Thomas,
Me give her the biggest piece,
   John Thomas,
And-a warra more you want,
   John Thomas?

"We all a combolow" means: "We're all friends."

92 THREE ACRE O' COFFEE

(Digging Song)

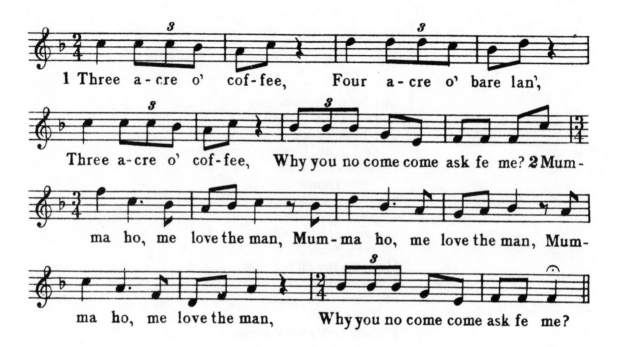

1 Three a-cre o' cof-fee, Four a-cre o' bare lan',
Three a-cre o' cof-fee, Why you no come come ask fe me? 2 Mumma ho, me love the man, Mum-ma ho, me love the man, Mumma ho, me love the man, Why you no come come ask fe me?

1 Three acre o' coffee,
  Four acre o' bare lan',
  Three acre o' coffee,
    Why you no come come ask fe me?

2 Mumma ho, me love the man,
  Mumma ho, me love the man,
  Mumma ho, me love the man,
    Why you no come come ask fe me?

A girl complains: "You boast you have land, why don't you come and ask
to marry me?"

93 ONCE I WAS A TRAV'LLER

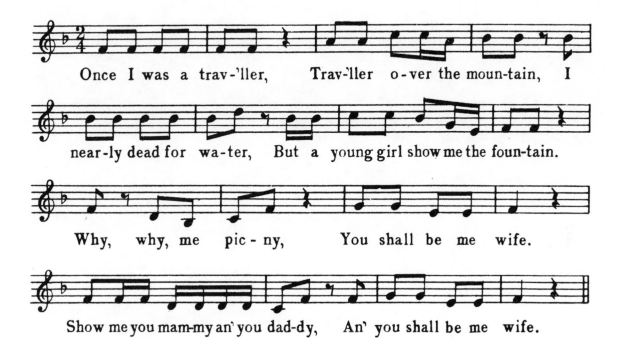

Once I was a trav-'ller, Trav-'ller o-ver the moun-tain, I near-ly dead for wa-ter, But a young girl show me the foun-tain. Why, why, me pic-ny, You shall be me wife. Show me you mam-my an' you dad-dy, An' you shall be me wife.

1 Once I was a trav'ller,
Trav'ller over the mountain,
I nearly dead for water,
But a young girl show me the fountain.
    Why, why, me picny,
    You shall be me wife.
    Show me you mammy an' you daddy,
    An' you shall be me wife.

2 I have another sister,
She blind she cannot see,
But, if you wish to court her,
You can come with me.
    Why, why, me picny,
    You shall be me wife.
    Show me you mammy an' you daddy,
    An' you shall be me wife.

TRINIDAD
AND
TOBAGO

94 ANANSI, PLAY FOR MA DOGOMA

(Bongo Dance-Song)

1 Play, boy, play, boy, Play fo' Ma Do-go-ma,

An-an-si, oh, Play fo' Ma Do-go-ma.

2 See how dem boys Are play fo' Ma Do-go-ma.

An-an-si, oh, Play fo' Ma Do-go-ma.

1 Play, boy, play, boy,
Play fo' Ma Dogoma. ⎫
Anansi, oh, ⎬ (2)
Play fo' Ma Dogoma. ⎭

2 See how dem boys
Are play fo' Ma Dogoma. ⎫
Anansi, oh, ⎬ (2)
Play fo' Ma Dogoma. ⎭

3 See how dem boys
Are dance for Ma Dogoma. ⎫
Anansi, oh, ⎬ (2)
Play fo' Ma Dogoma. ⎭

4 See how dem gals
Are dance fo' Ma Dogoma. ⎫
Anansi, oh, ⎬ (2)
Play fo' Ma Dogoma. ⎭

5 Play, boy, play, boy,
Play fo' Ma Dogoma. ⎫
Anansi, oh, ⎬ (2)
Play fo' Ma Dogoma. ⎭

Ma Dogoma is an African culture-heroine "without whose consent no-one can ever die." At death-wakes, offerings of food are made to her, and forfeit games and dances take place. Anansi is the house spider, the hero of many Negro tales.

95 WIND'ARD CAR'LINE

(Reel Dance-Song)

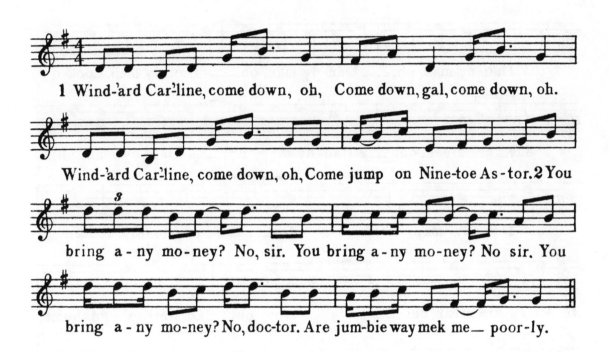

1 Wind-'ard Car'line, come down, oh, Come down, gal, come down, oh.

Wind-'ard Car'line, come down, oh, Come jump on Nine-toe As-tor. 2 You

bring a-ny mo-ney? No, sir. You bring a-ny mo-ney? No sir. You

bring a-ny mo-ney? No, doc-tor. Are jum-bie way mek me— poor-ly.

1 Wind'ard Car'line, come down, oh,
Come down, gal, come down, oh.
Wind'ard Car'line, come down, oh,
Come jump on Nine-toe Astor.

2 You bring any money? No, sir.
You bring any money? No, sir.
You bring any money? No, doctor.
Are jumbie way mek me poorly.

During the Reel-dance, the ancestral spirit of Ma Caroline from Windward, Tobago, is invited to come and take possession of the medium, Nine-toe Astor, and to pass on messages and advice. A sick person, having no money, has turned to the ancestors for a cure.

96   DANDY MAN, OH

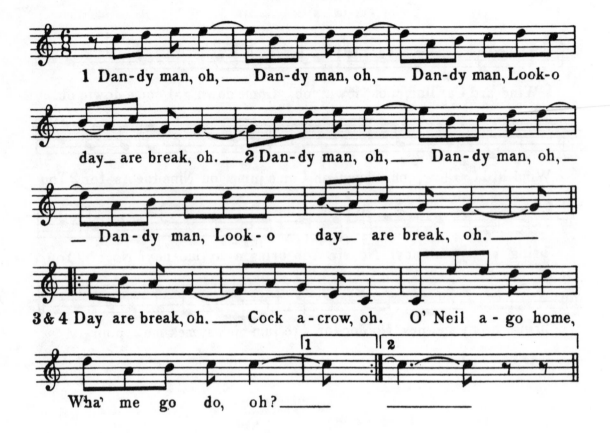

1 Dan-dy man, oh, ___ Dan-dy man, oh, ___ Dan-dy man, Look-o day___ are break, oh. ___ 2 Dan-dy man, oh, ___ Dan-dy man, oh, ___ Dan-dy man, Look-o day___ are break, oh. ___

3&4 Day are break, oh. ___ Cock a-crow, oh.   O' Neil a-go home, Wha' me go do, oh?___

1 Dandy man, oh,
Dandy man, oh,
Dandy man,
Look-o day are break, oh.

2 Dandy man, oh,
Dandy man, oh,
Dandy man,
Look-o day are break, oh.

3 Day are break, oh.
Cock a-crow, oh.
O'Neil a-go home,
Wha' me go do, oh?

4 Day are break, oh.
Cock a-crow, oh.
O'Neil a-go home,
Wha' me go do, oh?

During a Reel Dance, ancestral spirits are summoned from Africa with special songs and drumming. At day-break, the ancestors must leave the dance. The song is a lament at the departure of one of the spirits, O'Neil, here addressed by the affectionate term of "dandy man".

168

97 LEGGO ME HAN'

(Kalinda)

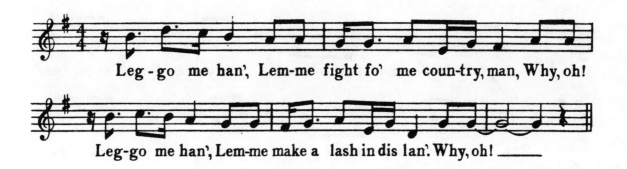

Leg-go me han', Lem-me fight fo' me coun-try, man, Why, oh!

Leg-go me han', Lem-me make a lash in dis lan'. Why, oh! ____

1 Leggo me han'.
  Lemme fight fo' me country, man,
  Why, oh!
  Leggo me han'.
  Lemme make a lash in dis lan',
  Why, oh!

2 Leggo me han'.
  Lemme fight fo' me country, man,
  Why, oh!
  Me mother will cry
  When she hear how she sweet man die,
  Why, oh!

3 Leggo me han'.
  Lemme fight fo' me country, man,
  Why, oh!
  Arima tonight,
  Sangre Grande tomorrow night,
  Why, oh!

Just before Carnival, the Kalinda stick-fighting bands roamed the country-side, engaging nightly with other bands, to win fame for themselves. Hence "Arima tonight, Sangre Grande tomorrow night."

98 CAP'N BAKER

(Kalinda)

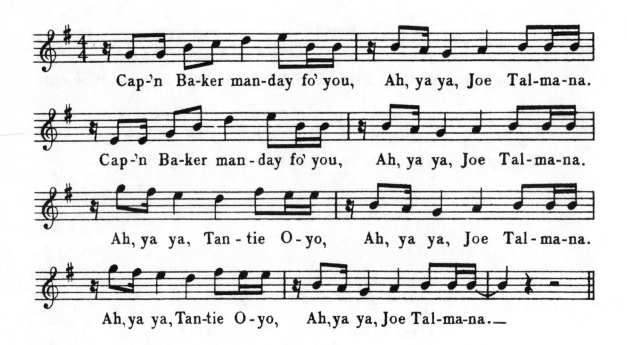

Cap'n Ba-ker man-day fo' you,   Ah, ya ya, Joe Tal-ma-na.

Cap-'n Ba-ker man-day fo' you,   Ah, ya ya, Joe Tal-ma-na.

Ah, ya ya, Tan-tie O-yo,   Ah, ya ya, Joe Tal-ma-na.

Ah, ya ya, Tan-tie O-yo,   Ah, ya ya, Joe Tal-ma-na.—

1 Cap'n Baker manday fo' you,
  Ah, ya ya, Joe Talmana.
  Cap'n Baker manday fo' you,
  Ah, ya ya, Joe Talmana.
  Ah, ya ya, Tantie Oyo,
  Ah, ya ya, Joe Talmana.
  Ah, ya ya, Tantie Oyo,
  Ah, ya ya, Joe Talmana.

manday: is calling

In 1881, Capt. Baker, police commandant in Trinidad, sought to stamp out the Kalinda stick-duelling game. Riots ensued, in which many were killed. Joe Talmana, a celebrated stick-fighter, had to be captured before the riot could be quelled. The song celebrates this folk-hero and his wife, Tantie Oyo.

170

99 EMMA

Em-ma, le' me 'lone, Le' me 'lone. Me no mar-ry yet, Le' me 'lone.

When me mar-ry, oh, Bell go ring. When me mar-ry, oh, Shell go blow.

Em-ma, le' me 'lone, Le' me 'lone. Me no mar-ry yet, Le' me 'lone.

1 Emma, le' me 'lone,
Le' me 'lone.
Me no marry yet,   } (2)
Le' me 'lone.
When me marry, oh,
Bell go ring.
When me marry, oh,
Shell go blow.
Emma, le' me 'lone,
Le' me 'lone.
Me no marry yet,
Le' me 'lone.

COLOMBIA

100 EL ZANCUDO

The Mosquito

1 E - ché mis per - ros al mon - te. El
u - no la - tió muy du - ro. El a - mo se fue a a - so -
mar Yer' un in - fe - liz zan - cu - do. 2 Cla - vé mi ro - dill - a en
tier - ra Ya - pun - té bi - en a - pun - tao, Y
fue tan grand' el ba - la - zo Que que - dó pa - ta - rri - bia - o.

1 Eché mis perros al monte.
  El uno latió muy duro.
  El amo se fue a asomar
  Y er' un infeliz zancudo.

2 Clavé mi rodilla en tierra
  Y apunté bien apuntao,
  Y fue tan grand' el balazo
  Que quedó patarribiao.

1 I sent my dogs in the thicket,
  And one of them started barking.
  When his master he looked around,
  It was but a poor mosquito.

2 I dug my heel in the ground, boys,
  And sighted along my rifle.
  The bullet hit him so hard, boys,
  That it fairly knocked him flying.

174

COLOMBIA

3 El zancudo cayó al mar
  Y se quedó en un remanso.
  Mil metros tenía de hondo
  Y una pata dabo al Cabo.

4 Pa matar ese animal
  Se tendió l'infantería
  Con quince ametralladoras
  Y un cañón d'infantería.

5 La carne d'este animal
  La mandaron pa Marmato
  Pesaba dos mil arrobas,
  Catorce libros y cuarto.

6 El sebo d'este animal
  Lo mandaron p'al Tabor.
  Eso hace quinientos años,
  Y todavía hay jabón.

7 Del cuero d'ese animal
  Salieron dos mil paraguas,
  Y un pedazo que sobró
  Se lu'hizo una vieja en naguas.

3 The mosquito fell in the ocean,
  Got stuck in the stagnant water,
  Full five hundred fathom deep,
  With one foot upon the headland.

4 To kill off this great mosquito,
  The infantry they lay down, boys,
  With fully fifteen machine-guns
  And an old infantry cannon.

5 The flesh of this great mosquito,
  They sent it up to Marmato,
  And it weighed about half a ton
  And forty pounds and a quarter.

6 The fat of this great mosquito,
  They sent it down to Tabor, lads,
  And that was five hundred years gone,
  And they don't need soap any more, lads.

7 The hide of this great mosquito
  Made two thousand fine umbrellas,
  And the little bit that was over
  Made a skirt for my grandmother.

V. M. and A. L. L.

101 EL PAJARILLO

The little Bird

Pa - ja - ri - llo men - sa - je - ro, Pa -
ja - ri - llo, pa - ja - ró, — A - quel án - gel que yo a -
do - ro, Pa - ja - ri - llo, pa - ja - ró. —

1 Pajarillo mensajero,
  Pajarillo, pajaró,
  Aquel ángel que yo adoro,
  Pajarillo, pajaró.

1 O pigeon, carrier pigeon,
  I'll send my sweetheart a message.
  I'll tell her that she's my angel.
  O pigeon, carrier pigeon.

2 Pajarillo que ayer tarde
  Cantabas tu libertad,
  Y agora por tu desgracia
  Te ves prisionero ya.

2 Just yesterday in the evening
  I heard you sing of your freedom.
  Today, dearest, to your sorrow,
  I see you are bound in prison.

3 Si yo fuera pajarillo,
  No me ocupara en volar.
  Me asentara en el camino
  Sólo por verte pasar.

3 Were I a red bird or swallow,
  I wouldn't care to fly, love.
  I'd sit alone by the roadside
  And watch you as you pass by, love.

4 Aquel pajarillo, madre,
  Que canta en el ramo verde,
  Ruégale a Dios que no cante
  Porque mi amor no se duerme.

4 You hear that little bird, mother,
  Among the leaves so green.
  Pray God she stops her singing;
  My sweetheart cannot sleep.

A. L. L.

102 LA CARTAGENA

Car - ta - ge - na del ol - vi - do, Puer - to

del mar ven - tu - ro - so, De las mu - je - res que -

ri - do Y de los hom - bres re - po - so, De las

mu - je - res que - ri - do Y de los hom-bres re - po - so.

1 Cartagena del olvido,
Puerto del mar venturoso,
De las mujeres querido } (2)
Y de los hombres reposo.

2 Saturnina y Zoila Toro
Que revuelan por el aidre.
Parecen dos hermanitas, } (2)
Hijas de una misma madre.

3 En Remedios yo tenía
Plata blanca en el carriel,
Y una negra que me daba } (2)
Quesito con mucha miel.

4 Quesito con mucha miel,
Yo lo tomo donde quiera,
Que pa eso'e los amores, } (2)
Yo canto en toda gallera.

1 Cartagena, who'd forget you?
You're the favourite with all women.
You're the jewel of the ocean } (2)
And a rest for weary seamen.

2 Saturnina and Zoila Toro,
When they take the air together,
Well, they look like two twin sisters, } (2)
Daughters of the selfsame mother.

3 Boys, I went up to Remedios
With a satchel full of money,
And a black girl there, she gave me } (2)
Little cheese with lots of honey.

4 Little cheese with lots of honey,
And I take it where I find it,
Because that's my way of loving, } (2)
So I crow in every cockpit.

A. L. L.

Zoila Toro was a negress of great fame (or notoriety) along the Cauca River
in south-western Colombia, during the nineteenth century. She appears in
many folk songs.

103 MI COMPADRE MONO

My friend Mister Monkey

Mi com-pa-dre Mo-no Tie-ne dos ca-mi-sas,

U-na que li'a-plan-chan, Yo-tra que li'a-

li-san. Va-lien-te mo-no Tan des-ca-ra-do Que no res-

pe-ta, Por ir a be-sar la no-via Be-só a la

sue-gra Y al-zó la ma-no Y le dio en la je-ta.

1 Mi compadre Mono
   Tiene dos camisas,
   Una que li'aplanchan,
   Y otra que li'alisan.
     Valiente mono
     Tan descarado
     Que no respeta,
     Por ir a besar la novia
     Besó a la suegra
     Y alzó la mano
     Y le dio en la jeta.

1 My friend Mister Monkey,
   He has got two shirts, boys.
   One is clean and ironed,
   T'other stained with dirt, boys.
     O valiant monkey,
     So bold and shameless,
     And disrespectful,
     Instead of kissing his sweetheart,
     Kisses her mother;
     Gives her a slap,
     Then gives her another.

2 Mi compadre mono
  Tiene dos calzones,
  Unos de bayeta
  Y otros sin botones.

3 Allá van los monos
  Por la travesía
  A alcanzar el baile
  De Juana Maria
    Valiente mono
    Tan descarado
    Que no respeta,
    Por ir a besar la novia
    Besó a la suegra
    Y alzó la mano
    Y le dio en la jeta.

2 My friend Mister Monkey
  Has two pairs of trousers,
  One pair made of flannel,
  One pair without buttons.

3 Yonder go the monkeys,
  Skipping down the alley,
  Hoping they can get to
  Dona Juana's party.
    O valiant monkey,
    So bold and shameless
    And disrespectful,
    Instead of kissing his sweetheart,
    Kisses her mother,
    Gives her a slap,
    Then gives her another.

A. L. L.

104 VAN CANTANDO POR LA SIERRA

O'er the mountain they go singing

1 Van can - tan - do por la sier - ra   Con hon -
da me-lan-co-lí - a, ____ U - nos can-tos de mi
tier - ra ____ Cuan - do   va   mu-rien-do el día - a.

2 Ti - ñe el a-zul ho - ri - zon - te   U - na lu-mi-no-sa
fran - ja, ____ Que da   a   los lla - nos y al mon - te
Sua-ve co-lor de na - ran - ja, ____ Sua-ve co - lor de na - ran - ja.

1 Van cantando por la sierra
Con honda melancolía,
Unos cantos de mi tierra
Cuando va muriendo el día. } (2)

1 O'er the mountain they go singing.
Their voices seem to be crying,
Singing songs of my home country
As the day is slowly dying.

2 Tiñe el azul horizonte
Una luminosa franja,
Que da a los llanos y al monte
Suave color de naranja. } (2)

2 And across the blue horizon
Spreads a growing fringe of colour,
Giving both the plain and the mountain
The gentle hue of an orange.

3 Canta el ave enamorada
En el follaje sombrío,
Y murmura en la enramada
Su extraño lenguaje al río. } (2)

3 The enamoured bird is singing
Among the thick shady foliage,
And the strange tongue of the river
Murmurs in the tangled branches.

4 Se escucha el suave concento
De hojarascas y bejucos,
Mientras que se lleva el viento
El eco de mis bambucos. } (2)

4 We can hear the gentle concord
Of the dry leaves and lianas,
While the wind bears across the landscape
The echo of my *bambuco*.
                              V. M. and A. L. L.

VENEZUELA

105 ADORAR AL NIÑO

Come, hasten, shepherds

(Villancico)

1 A - do - rar al   ni - ño   Cor - re - mos pas - to - res,
2 A - do - ro el mis - te - rio   De la Tri - ni - dad, ___

Que es - tá en el por - tal ___   Lle - ve - mos - le   flo - res.
Que son tres per - so - nas Y es un Dios no   más. ___

Que es - tá en el por - tal ___   Lle - ve - mos - le   flo - res.
Que son tres per - so - nas Y es un Dios no   más. ___

3 U - na pa - lo - mi - ta   A - nnun - ció a Ma - rí - a

Que en su se - no   san - to   El en - car - na - rí - a,

Que en su se - no san - to   El en - car - na - rí - a.

VENEZUELA

1 Adorar al niño
  Corremos pastores, } (2)
  Que está en el portal } (2)
  Llevemosle flores.

2 Adoro el misterio } (2)
  De la Trinidad,
  Que son tres personas } (2)
  Y es un Dios no más.

3 Una palomita } (2)
  Annunció a María
  Que en su seno santo } (2)
  El encarnaría.

1 Come, hasten, shepherds, } (2)
  And adore the Baby.
  Let us bring Him flowers, } (2)
  Who lies in the manger.

2 Let us worship, shepherds, } (2)
  The Trinity most holy,
  Which is persons three } (2)
  And is one God only.

3 'Twas a snow-white dove } (2)
  Brought the news to Mary.
  In her holy womb } (2)
  Lay the princely Baby.

V. M. and A. L. L.

106 LA CORONA

The Crown

1 Esa es tu corona.
  Corona bella,
  Toda rodeada
  De las estrellas.

2 Ese es tu pelo.
  Es pelo rubio
  Donde se agarró el Niño
  Cuando el diluvio.

1 Here's your crown, my Lady,
  Crown of the finest.
  Behold, all around it
  Bright stars are shining.

2 Here is your hair, Lady,
  ʹFine hair and flaxen,
  That the Infant Jesus
  Seized when the Flood came.

VENEZUELA

3 Esa es tu frente,
  Frente de plata.
  El platero que la hizo
  Nada le falta.

4 Esas tus cejas
  Arca les puso,
  Donde anduvo el Niño
  Cuando el diluvio.

5 Ese tu cuerpo,
  Cuerpo de gloria,
  Donde te pedimos
  Misericordia.

6 Esos tus brazos
  Son dos corales
  Con que abrazaste
  Todos los mortales.

7 Esos tus pechos
  Son dos diamantes
  Con que alimentaste
  Aquel Niño Infante.

3 Next, here is your forehead,
  Forehead of silver,
  And the smith who wrought it
  Was the most skilful.

4 And these are your eyebrows.
  Of them the Ark was made,
  That the Infant Jesus
  Sailed when the Flood came.

5 And this is your body,
  Body of glory,
  Before which we beg you
  For your sweet mercy.

6 These are your arms, Lady,
  They are two corals,
  With which you're embracing
  All of us mortals.

7 These are your breasts, Lady,
  They are two diamonds
  With which you did nourish
  Your Holy Infant.

                    V. M. and A. L. L.

107 TONO DE VELORIO DE CRUZ
Watch-Night Song

1 En un jar-din de-li-cio-so A-dán y E-va se ha-

lla-ban. En un jar-din de-li-cio-so A-dán y E-va se ha-

lla-ban. En un lla-ban. 2 Cuan-do él mi-ró que pe-có, ¡Ay!

VENEZUELA

A-dán sa-lió de ca - rre - ra. Cuan-do el mi-ró que pe-

ca - rre - ra.

có, ¡Ay!_ A - dán sa-lió de ca - rre - ra.____

ca - rre - ra.

Hmmm.

Hmm Hmmm. Ah, y a-do-rar al que na - ció, Na-na nay.

Hmmm.

1 En un jardin delicioso
  Adán y Eva se hallaban.
  En un jardin delicioso
  Adán y Eva se hallaban. } (2)

1 In a green delicious garden
  Eve and Adam went a-walking.
  In a green delicious garden
  Eve and Adam went a-walking. } (2)

2 Cuando él miró que pecó, ¡Ay!
  Adán salió de carrera.
  Cuando él miró que pecó, ¡Ay!
  Adán salió de carrera. } (2)
    Ah, y adorar al que nació,
    Nana nay.

2 When he saw that he had sinned, Ay!
  Adam quickly sought a refuge.
  And when he saw that he had sinned,
                              Ay!
  Then he quickly sought a refuge. } (2)
    Ah, let us all adore the Babe,
    Nana nay.

A. L. L.

187

108 LA BURRIQUITA
The Little Donkey

Guitar

Ya vie-ne la bu-rri-qui-ta,— Ya vie-ne do-mes-ti - cá. Ya cá. No le te-man a la bu-rra Que no es la bu-rra ma-niá. No le niá. Ay sí, ay no, Ma-ri-qui-ta me re-ga-ló Un ca-na-rio que can-ta-ba Los ver-sos del Ni-ño Dios. Un ca- Dios.

VENEZUELA

1 Ya viene la burriquita, ⎱ (2)
  Ya viene domesticá. ⎰
  No le teman a la burra ⎱ (2)
  Que no es la burra maniá. ⎰
  Ay sí, ay no,
  Mariquita me regaló
  Un canario que cantaba ⎱ (3)
  Los versos del Niño Dios. ⎰

1 Now here comes the little donkey, ⎱ (2)
  He's such a nice quiet beast. ⎰
  Don't be frightened of the donkey ⎱ (2)
  For he's not a horrid ghost. ⎰
  Oh, yes. Oh, no.
  Mariquita gave to her beau
  A canary bird that sings a song ⎱ (3)
  About the Child of God. ⎰

V. M. and A. L. L.

'La burra maniá' is a nightmare animal whose menacing role in Latin American folklore is similar to that of the Big Bad Wolf in North European tradition.

189

109 EL MAMPULORIO

1 Por las á - ni-mas ben - di-tas Que es-tán en el pur-ga-

to-rio, A-quí e-stá la ve - la del mam-pu-lo - rio, A-quí e-stá la ro-

- sa del mam-pu-lo - rio, A-quí e-stá el ci - ga - rro del mam-pu-lo-

- rio, A-quí es-tá la tam-bo - ra del mam-pu - lo-

rio, A-quí e - stá la gui-ta - rra del mam-pu - lo-

rio, A-quí e - stá la ma-ra - ca del man-pu - lo - rio.

2 Ay, mi po - lli - to sa-lió a la ca - lle Y le rue-go a

VENEZUELA

Dios Que na-die lo ha - lle, na-die lo ha - lle, Na-die lo ha al ﹩ *a FIN*

- lle, na-die lo ha - lle, Na-die lo ha - lleA -qui e-stá la ro -

1 Por las ánimas benditas
  Que están en el purgatorio,
  Aquí está la vela
    del mampulorio,
  Aquí está la rosa
    del mampulorio,
  Aquí está el cigarro
    del mampulorio,
  Aquí está la tambora
    del mampulorio,
  Aquí está la guitarra
    del mampulorio,
  Aquí está la maraca
    del mampulorio.

2 Ay, mi pollito salió a la calle
  Y le ruego a Dios
  Que nadie lo halle,
    nadie lo halle,
  Nadie lo halle,
    nadie lo halle,
  Nadie lo halle.
  Aquí está la rosa
    del mampulorio, etc.

1 Oh, for all the blessed spirits
  Now in Purgatory residing,
  This is the candle
    of mampulorio,
  This is the rose of
    the mampulorio,
  Here's the cigar of
    the mampulorio,
  And here is the drum of
    the mampulorio,
  And here's the guitar of
    the mampulorio,
  And here's the maraca
    of mampulorio.

2 My little chicken ran in the roadway
  And I pray to God that
  No-one may find it,
    no-one may find it,
  No-one may find it,
    no-one may find it,
  No-one may find it.
  This is the rose of
    the mampulorio, etc.

                              A. L. L.

The song accompanies a forfeit-game played at Negro wakes in Miranda
Province. The player tries to blow out a candle waved in front of his face,
at the same time as he names various objects dropped into a hat on his knees.

110 AMALIA ROSA

(Golpe)

Guitar

1 De Ma - ra - cai - bo sa - lie - ron
2 To - ma, ni - ña, es - te pu - ñal.

Dos pa - lo - mi - tas vo - lan - do.   A la Guai - ra vo - la -
Ab - ri - me por un cos - ta - do,   Pa' que veas mi co - ra -

rán,   A la Guai - ra vo - la - rán, ay, ¿Pe - ro a Ma - ra - cai - bo
zón,   Pa' que veas mi co - ra - zón, ay, Con el tu - yo re - tra -

cuan - do?   3 Ma - rí - a   me dió u - na   cin - ta Y
ta - do.

Ro - sa me la qui - tó.   A - ma - lia pe - lió con

e - lla Por - que Jua - na,   por - que Jua - na se en - o - jó.

4 Ya se jun - ta - ron las cua - tro   Que son las que quie - ro

yo, __ A - ma - lia, A - ma - lia, A - ma - lia,   A - ma - lia, A - ma - lia,

VENEZUELA

Ro-sa, E-sa es la que yo me lle - vo. E-sa es la que yo me
lle - vo Por - que es la más bue - na mo -
1 Em   A7   2 G   A7   D
za. —————— - za. ——————

1 De Maracaibo salieron
Dos palomitas volando.
A La Guaira volarán,
A La Guaira volarán, ay,
¿Pero a Maracaibo cuando?

2 Toma, niña, este puñal.
Abrime por un costado,
Pa'que veas mi corazón,
Pa'que veas mi corazón, ay,
Con el tuyo retratado.

3 María me dió una cinta
Y Rosa me la quitó.
Amalia pelió con ella
Porque Juana, porque Juana se enojó.⎬(2)

4 Ya se juntaron las cuatro
Que son las que quiero yo,
Amalia, Amalia, Amalia,
Amalia, Amalia, Rosa,
Esa es la que yo me llevo.
Esa es la que yo me llevo
Porque es la más buena moza.⎬(2)

1 One fine day from Maracaibo
Two white pigeons they went flying.
For La Guaira they are bound,
For La Guaira they are bound,
But when, ah, when to Maracaibo?

2 Oh, my darling, take this dagger.
With it open up my left side
And then you will see my heart.
And then you will see my heart, love,
With your own engraved upon it.

3 Maria gave me a ribbon.
Rosa took it away.
Amalia started to fight her
Because Juana, Juana got into a rage.⎬(2)

4 Now the four are come together.
They're the ones that I love best.
Amalia, Amalia, Amalia,
Amalia, Amalia, Rose
Is the one I'm taking with me,
She's the one I'm taking because
Of them all she is the sweetest.

V. M. and A. L. L.

111 SE FUÉ VOLANDO

They have flown away

(Fulía)

1 To-das   las flo-res mar - cha - ron,   Se fué vo-
2 En bus-ca del tu - li - pan___

lan - do(,)   U - na   ma - ña-na de e - ne - ro.
Y   la   flor   de 'por ti   mue - ro.'

O - le   le   le   le, ___   O - le   le_ le - le,

E - o,___   o - le   le   le - le. ___

1 Todas las flores marcharon,
   Se fué volando
  Una mañana de enero.
   Ole le lele,
   Ole le lele,
   Eo, ole le lele.

2 En busca del tulipan
   Se fué volando,
  Y la flor de 'por ti muero'.
   Ole le lele,
   Ole le lele,
   Eo, ole le lele.

3 Todas las flores marcharon,
   Se fué volando
  Una mañana de abril.
   Ole le lele,
   Ole le lele,
   Eo, ole le lele.

4 En busca del tulipan
   Se fué volando,
  Que no estaba en el pensil.
   Ole le lele,
   Ole le lele,
   Eo, ole le lele.

1 All the flowers now will leave us,
   They have flown away
  On a January morning.
   Ole le lele,
   Ole le lele,
   Eo, ole le lele.

2 They've gone looking for the tulip,
   They have flown away,
  And the flower called 'Por ti muero'.
   Ole le lele,
   Ole le lele,
   Eo, ole le lele.

3 All the flowers now will leave us,
   They have flown away
  On a sunny April morning.
   Ole, le lele,
   Ole le lele,
   Eo, ole le lele.

4 They've gone looking for the tulip,
   They have flown away
  Since it wasn't in the garden.
   Ole le lele,
   Ole le lele,
   Eo, ole le lele.

A.L.L.

112 SANGUÉO

¡E jé jé! Yo di - vi - sé un li - rio blan - co Que en el
cie - lo se mi - ra - ba Con los ra - yos de la lu - na.

Drum  *simile*

1 ¡E jé jé!
  Yo divisé un lirio blanco
  Que en el cielo se miraba } (2)
  Con los rayos de la luna.

1 Eh hey hey!
  I can see a lily shining
  As she looks up to the heavens } (2)
  In the pale light of the moonbeams.

A. L. L.

113 EL CARITE

The Fish

1 A - yer sa - lió___ la lan-cha Nue-va Es-

par - ta.___ Sa-lió con-fia-da___ a re-cor-rer los ma - res.

En-con-tró un pez___ de fuer-zas muy li - je - ro, Que a-

ga-rra los an-zue-los y re-vien-ta los gua-ra - les.___

ra - les. Co - mo la cos-ta es bo -

ni - ta Yo me ven - go di-vir-tien-do Pe - ro___

___ me vie-ne si - guien-do De fue-rau - na pi - ra -

gui - ta. Co - mo gui - ta.___ 2 A - yer sa -

VENEZUELA

1 Ayer salió la lancha Nueva Esparta.
Salió confiada a recorrer los mares.
Encontró un pez de fuerzas muy lijero,
Que agarra los anzuelos y revienta los guarales.
  Como la costa es bonita
  Yo me vengo divirtiendo
  Pero me viene siguiendo
  De fuera una piraguita.

2 Ayer salimos muy temprano a pescar
Nos fuimos juntos todos los pescadores
Y entre las olas lo vimos saltando
Que iba persiguiendo a los voladores.
  Como la costa etc.

3 Un marinero al verlo se alegró
A este sabroso pescado de los mares
Y en seguida les dijo a los muchachos
Preparen los arpones y tiren los guarales.
  Como la costa etc.

4 En los ramales del coco lo pescamos
En lo profundo del mar donde vivía
Y lo pescamos en la lancha Nueva Esparta
Para presentarlo hoy con alegría.
  Como la costa etc.

5 Señores todos les damos las gracias
Los pescadores se van a marchar
Nos despedimos con este Carite
Que les presentamos en este lugar.

1 The other day set sail the *Nuev' Esparta,*
And with high hopes there she scudded o'er the ocean.
She met a fish, a fish so very cunning,
He tangled all our lines, boys, and caused us much commotion.
  Ay, señor, our coast is pleasant.
  I was sailing at my leisure
  When I chanced to spy a canoe
  Far away but coming after.

2 Oh, it was early, early in the morning
When we bold fishermen all went out together.
Among the waves, 'twas there we saw him leaping
And knew that he was chasing the lively baracuda.
  Ay, señor, etc.

3 A sailor spied him and cried out for joy, lads,
To see this tasty great monster of the ocean.
"All hands on deck!" he shouted to his shipmates,
"Get ready with your harpoons and heave hard on the rope-lines!"
  Ay, señor, etc.

4 Across the gulf with all its twisting currents,
And in the deeps where he always went for shelter,
We chased that fish all in the *Nuev' Esparta,*
So now we can present him, and with the greatest pleasure.
  Ay, señor, etc.

5 Good people all, it's time for us to leave you.
We fishermen, we give thanks for your attention.
We say goodbye with our monster carite,
Which with your kind permission, we proudly have presented.
                    V. M. and A. L. L.

114 QUE EL CANTAR TIENE SENTIDO

A song has its meaning

(Polo Margariteño)

* The letters correspond to the chords played by the cuatro, or small guitar.

VENEZUELA

mo-ra más que el dí - a; __ Mi á - ni-ma su - til nun - ca se

sa - cia, __ La no-che me e-na - mo-ra más que el

dí - a; Y Mi á-ni-ma su - til nun-ca se sa - cia,

De gus - tar su i-ne - fable po - e - sí - a __

__ Y en-ca - re - cer __ su ex-cel-sa a-ris-to - cra - cia. __

1 Que el cantar tiene sentido, (2)
  Entendimiento y razón,
  Que el cantar tiene sentido,
  (¡Dale, duro!)
  Entendimiento y razón,
  La buena pronunciación ⎫
  (¡Oye, Julián!)   ⎬ (2)
  Del instrumento al oído.   ⎭

1 Oh, a song it has its meaning, (2)
  Understanding and reason.
  Oh, a song it has its meaning,
  (Hit it hard!)
  Understanding and reason,
  The good pronunciation   ⎫
  (Listen, Julian!)   ⎬ (2)
  Between instrument and hearing.⎭

2 La noche me enamora más que el día; ⎫ (2)
  Mi ánima sutil nunca se sacia,   ⎭
  De gustar su inefable poesía
  Y encarecer su excelsa aristocracia.

2 The night delights me better than   ⎫
                         the daytime; ⎬ (2)
  And my subtle mind is never sated   ⎭
  With the taste of its prodigious poetry,
  And with extolling its lofty aristocracy.

A. L. L.

BRAZIL

115 LA NAU *CATARINETA*

The ship *Catarineta*

(Romance)

Faz vint' um a-nos e um di - a Que an-da-mos n'on-das do mar, Bo-tan-do so-las de mô-lho, O to-li - na, Pa - ra de noi - te jan - tar.

1 Faz vint' um anos e um dia
Que andamos n'ondas do mar,
Botando solas de môlho, O tolina, } (2)
Para de noite jantar.

2 A sola era tão dura
Que a não podemos tragar.
Foi-se vendo pela sorte, O tolina,
Quem se havia de matar.
Logo foi cair a sorte, O tolina,
No capitão general.

3 Sobe, sobe, meu gageiro,
Meu gageirinho real;
Vê se vês terras d'Espanha, O tolina, } (2)
Areias de Portugal.

4 Não vejo terras d'Espanha,
Areias de Portugal.
Vejo sete espadas nuas, O tolina, } (2)
Tôdas para te matar.

5 Sobe, sobe, meu gageiro,
Meu gageirinho real;
Olha prá estrêla do norte, O tolina, } (2)
Para poder nos guiar.

6 Alvistas, meu capitão!
Alvistas, meu general!
Avistei terras d'Espanha, O tolina, } (2)
Areias de Portugal!

1 It's twenty-one years and over
We sailed upon the salt sea,
Until we were boiling our boots, O
tolina, } (2)
For we had nought else to eat.

2 The leather it was so hard, lads,
We couldn't eat it at all,
So we cast lots for to see, O tolinda,
Which of the crew we should kill,
And on our captain so bold, O tolina,
The lot it happened to fall.

3 Oh, climb aloft then, my topman,
My little topman so royal!
Do you see the land of Spain, O
tolina, } (2)
The sands of fair Portugal?

4 The land of Spain I don't see, sir,
Nor sands of fair Portugal,
But I see six naked swords, O tolina, } (2)
And you're the one they would kill.

5 Aloft again, O my topman,
My little topman so bright!
The northern star will appear, O
tolina, } (2)
And you may guide us aright.

6 Good news, good news, O my captain!
Good news, my shipmates and all!
I see the coastline of Spain, O tolina, } (2)
The sands of fair Portugal!

115 La Nau *Catarineta* (*continued*)

7 Também avistei três moças
  Sentadas num parreiral;
  Duas cosendo setim, O tolina,
  Outro calçando dedal. } (2)

8 Tôdas três são minhas filhas,
  Ai, quem m'as dera abraçar!
  A mas bonita de tôdas, O tolina,
  Para contigo casar. } (2)

9 Eu não quero sua filha
  Que lhe custou a criar.
  Quero a nau *Catarineta*, O tolina,
  Para nela navegar. } (2)

10 Tenho meu cavalo branco,
  Como não há outro igual;
  Dar-to-ei de presente, O tolina,
  Para nêle passear. } (2)

11 Eu não quero su cavalo,
  Que lhe custou a criar.
  Quero a nau *Catarineta*, O tolina,
  Para nela navegar. } (2)

12 Tenho meu palácio nobre,
  Como não há outro assim;
  Com suas telhas de prata, O tolina,
  Suas portas de marfim. } (2)

13 Eu não quero su palácio,
  Tão caro de edificar.
  Quero a nau *Catarineta*, O tolina,
  Para nela navegar. } (2)

14 A nau *Catarineta*, amigo,
  É d'El-Rei de Portugal.
  Ou eu não serei quem sou, O tolina,
  Ou El-Rei te há de dar. } (2)

15 Desce, desce, meu gageiro,
  Meu gageirinho real!
  Já viste terras d'Espanha, O tolina,
  Areias de Portugal! } (2)

7 Likewise I see three young maidens
  A-sitting under a vine.
  One of them puts on her thimble
           tolina, } (2)
  Two sew their satin so fine.

8 The three girls, they are my daughters,
  Three little stars of my life.
  The prettiest of them all, O tolina,
  Shall be your own wedded wife. } (2)

9 It's not your daughter I care for,
  Who cost you so much to raise.
  I want the *Catarineta*, tolina,
  In her the world I would sail. } (2)

10 Oh, I have a snow-white stallion.
  There's not another so fine;
  To ride where'er you've a mind.
  And you may have him for yours, O } (2)
           tolina,

11 It's not your stallion I care for,
  That cost you so much to raise.
  I want the *Catarineta*, tolina,
  In her the world I would sail. } (2)

12 Oh, I have a noble palace,
  It's like you'll never behold.
  For it has portals of marble, tolina,
  And roofs of silver and gold. } (2)

13 It's not your palace I care for,
  That cost you so much to build.
  I want the *Catarineta*, tolina,
  To sail in around the world. } (2)

14 The good ship *Catarineta*,
  She is the king's, as you know.
  Either I'm not who I am, O tolina,
  Or he will give her to you. } (2)

15 Come down, Oh come down, my
           topman,
  My little topman so royal!
  I see the bright land of Spain, O
           tolina, } (2)
  The sands of fair Portugal!

A. L. L.

116 COMO PODE VIVIR O PEIXE

How can a fish live

(Coreto)

Co - mo po - de vi - vir o pei - xe Sem ser den - tro d'á - gua

fria? As - sim pos - so eu vi - vir_ Sem a tu - a com - pa -

nhia, Sem a tu - a. sem a tu - a, Sem a tu - a com - pa - nhia.

1 Como pode vivir o peixe
  Sem ser dentro d'água fria?
  Assim posso eu vivir
  Sem a tua companhia.
    Sem a tua, sem a tua,
    Sem a tua companhia.

1 Tell me, how can a little fish live
  Without water fresh and clear?
  Just the same would I live, darling,
  When my sweetheart is not here.
    When my sweetheart, when my
                  sweetheart,
    When my sweetheart is not here.

2 Os pastores desta aldeia
  De mim fazem zombaria,
  Por me ver andar chorando, (2)
    Sem a tua, sem a tua,
    Sem a tua companhia.

2 All the shepherds in our village
  Like to make a game of me,
  When they see me sadly mourning
  Far from your sweet company.
    Far from your sweet, far from your
                  sweet,
  Far from your sweet company.

A. L. L.

117 TENHO UM VESTIDO NOVO

I have got a new dress

(Fandango)

1 Te-nho um ves - ti - do no - vo Que me deu meu na - mo -

ra - do Pra pas-seá na do - min - go Com meu bem lá dou-tro

la - do. 2 Tu-do is - so a -con-te - ce A quem ca -

sá con-tra von - ta-de, A quem ca - sá con-tra von -

ta - de Se o ma-ri-do tá no sí-tio A mu-lher tá na ci-da-de.

3 Vou-me em-bo - ra prá ci - da - de Vou cui - dá de pes-ca -

ri - a, Ar-ran-já um ca-ma-ra-da Prá pes-cá de noi-te e

di - a. 4 E cer - to que vou-me em-bo - ra, Que vou-me em-

bo - ra prá ci - da-de. De mim não te-nhas cui - da - do!

BRAZIL

1 Tenho um vestido novo Que me deu meu namorado Pra passeá no domingo Com meu bem lá doutro lado.	1 Well, I have got a new dress, And it's a gift from my sweet lover, To wear on Sundays when I'm with him, And not with that other.
2 Tudo isso acontece A quem casá contra vontade, A quem casá contra vontade, Se o marido tá no sítio A mulher tá na cidade.	2 And all this is sure to be so If a girl weds against her wishes, If she weds against her wishes, And the husband's on his farm And his young wife is in the city.
3 Vou-me embora prá cidade, Vou cuidá de pescaria, Arranjá um camarada Prá pescá de noite e dia.	3 Well now, I'm off to the city, Off to look after a fish-pond, And to join up with a comrade And go fishing all the night long.
4 E certo que vou-me embora, Que vou-me embora prá cidade. De mim não tenhas cuidado!	4 Yes, sure, I am bound to leave you, I'm bound away to that old city, For on me you have no pity!

A. L. L.

118 DA BAHIA ME MANDARAM

From Bahia someone sent me

(Coco)

Da Ba - hi - a___ me man-da-ram U - ma ca - mi -

___ sa bor - da - da. Na a - ber-tu - ra da ca - mi - sa___ Ti-nha o

no - me da sa-fa-da, Li - o - né! O - lê Li - o - né! Ca-dê Li - a -

nô? Qu'eu ta-va na va - ran - da__ Quan-do a mo-re-na pas-sô, Li-o - né !

BRAZIL

1 Da Bahia me mandaram
Uma camisa bordada.
Na abertura da camisa
Tinha o nome da safada,
Lioné!

2 Olê Lioné!
Cadê Lianô?
Qu'eu tava na varanda
Quando a morena passô,
Lioné!

1 From Bahia someone sent me
An embroidered shift of linen.
On the bosom of this garment
Was the name of that young villain,
Lionel!

2 Ole, Lionel!
Where is Lionel?
I was on the verandah
When the brownskin girl went by,
Lionel!

A. L. L.

119 TRISTE VIDA É DO MARUJO

Tris - te vi - da é do ma - ru - jo____ Qual
de - las a mais can - sa - da,____ Que pe - la tris - te sol -
da - da Pas - sa tor - men - tos, Pas - sa tor - men - tos, Don, don.

1 Triste vida é do marujo
  Qual delas a mais cansada,
  Que pela triste soldada
    Passa tormentos, (2)
    Don, don.

2 Andar à chuva e aos ventos,
  Quer de verão quer de inverno;
  Parecem o próprio inferno
    As tempestades! (2)
    Don, don.

3 As nossas necessidades
  Nos obrigam a navegar,
  A passar tempos no mar,
    E aguaceiros. (2)
    Don, don.

1 A sailor's life is a sad one,
  And has been all through the ages,
  And for his pitiful wages,
    He suffers torments, (2)
    Ding dong.

2 Out in the wind and the weather,
  Alike in summer and winter,
  Aye, they are hellishly bitter,
    Those ocean tempests, (2)
    Ding dong.

3 Necessity drives us to it,
  Else we would not have the notion
  To spend our time on the ocean
    Among the rain-storms, (2)
    Ding dong.

BRAZIL

4 Quando sossegados estamos
　No rancho a descansar,
　Então é que ouço gritar:
　　Oh! leva arriba! (2)
　　Don, don.

5 O mestre logo se estriba,
　Bradando desta maneira:
　Moços ferra a cavadeira
　　E o joanete! (2)
　　Don, don.

6 Mais me valera ser visto
　A porta de um botequim,
　Do que ver agora o fim
　　Da minha vida. (2)
　　Don, don.

7 Quando parece comprida
　A noite pra descansar
　Então e que ouço tocar
　　Certa matraca. (2)
　　Don, don.

8 O sono logo se atraca
　Meu coração logo treme
　Em cuidar que hei de ir ao leme
　　Estar duas horas. (2)
　　Don, don.

9 Lembram-me certas senhoras
　Com quem eu tratei em terra,
　Que me estão fazendo guerra
　　Ao meu dinheiro. (2)
　　Don, don.

10 Foi um velho marinheiro
　Que inventou esta cantiga,
　Embarcado tôda a vida
　　Sem ter dinheiro. (2)
　　Don, don.

4 We come below to the foc'sle,
　And to our bunks we're retiring,
　We hear the first mate a-crying:
　　Up here and haul, lads! (2)
　　Ding dong.

5 The captain he is excited,
　He's shouting all kinds of orders.
　Hey, raise her up there, you lubbers!
　　Set your t'ga'nts'l! (2)
　　Ding dong.

6 Well now, I'd rather be seeing
　The painted door of a tavern
　Than be facing the vision
　　Of my life's end, boys, (2)
　　Ding dong.

7 As in my bunk I am dreaming
　A long night's rest is before me,
　That's when I hear them sounding
　　That well-known rattle, (2)
　　Ding dong.

8 Straightway my dream disappears, lads,
　Straightway my heart begins shaking
　To think the helm I'll be taking
　　At two in the morning, (2)
　　Ding dong.

9 I recall certain young women
　That I have met when ashore, lads,
　Thinking of how they waged war, lads,
　　Upon my money, (2)
　　Ding dong.

10 This song was made by a sailor
　Who took a tragical notion
　To spend his life on the ocean,
　　And made no money, (2)
　　Ding dong.

A. L. L.

120 VEM CÁ, CABELEIRA

Come here, Cabeleira

(Romance)

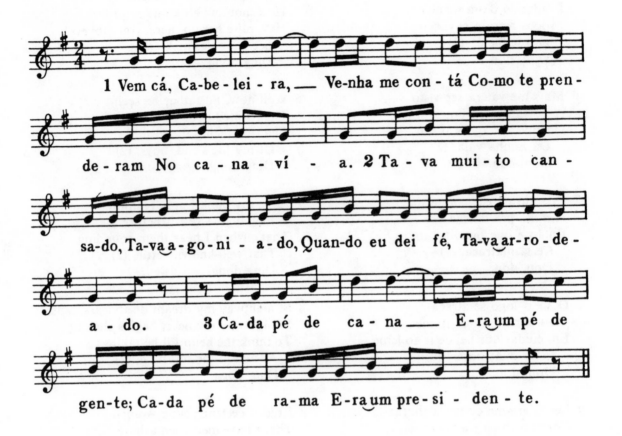

1 Vem cá, Ca-be-lei - ra, ___ Ve-nha me con - tá Co-mo te pren-
de - ram No ca - na - ví - a. 2 Ta - va mui - to can-
sa-do, Ta-va a-go-ni - a - do, Quan-do eu dei fé, Ta-va ar-ro-de-
a - do. 3 Ca-da pé de ca - na ___ E-ra um pé de
gen-te; Ca-da pé de ra-ma E-ra um pre-si - den - te.

BRAZIL

1 Vem cá, Cabeleira,
  Venha me contá
  Como te prenderam
  No canavía.

2 Tava muito cansado,
  Tava agoniado,
  Quando eu dei fé,
  Tava arrodeado.

3 Cada pé de cana
  Era um pé de gente;
  Cada pé de rama
  Era um presidente.

1 Come here, Cabeleira,
  Come and tell to me
  How it was they caught you
  In the old cane-field.

2 I was very weary
  And in misery
  When I realized,
  They'd surrounded me.

3 Every foot of cane, boys,
  Was a crowd of men;
  Every foot of stalk, boys,
  Was a president.

                A. L. L.

In north-eastern Brazil, 'Cabeleira' ('Long-hair') was the nickname of José Gomes, an eighteenth century bandit. 'Presidente' here means police-president.

121 COLÔNIA, USINA CATENDE

Colonia, and hungry Catende

1 Colônia, usina Catende,
  Roçadim de seu Mende,
  Pirangi de seu Cando,
  Neste mundo eu ando
  Cumprindo uma sina,
  Que inté nas usina
  Já tou trabalhando!
    Ai! Baiana,
    Baiana que é que há?
    Ou! Baiana,
    Baiana, meu amor!

1 Colonia, and hungry Catende,
  Mendes' Rocadim Central,
  Seu Candido's Pirangi,
  And so I'm drifting still,
  Fulfilling my sad lot,
  Since all the work I've got
  Is in these sugar-mills.
    Ah, Baiana,
    Baiana, Lord above!
    Oh, Baiana,
    Baiana, be my love!

BRAZIL

2 Palmares, Ribeirão, Escada,
  Eu tenho uma namorada
  Que me deu um broquel;
  A volta é cruel
  Na namoração
  No apêrto de mão
  Foi s'embora o anel!

3 Da usina sou cabo de esteira
  Trabalho nas caldeira
  Da luz do motor,
  Sou distilador
  De esprito de vinho,
  Entendo um pouquinho
  De cunzinhadô!

4 Baiana só quer beber vinho
  Zinebra Fokinho,
  Conhaque e licor;
  Cigarro Condor
  Marca Lafayette,
  Tomar deforéte
  Quando faz calor.
    Ai! Baiana,
    Baiana que é que há?
    Ou! Baiana,
    Baiana, meu amor!

2 Palmares, Riberão, Escada,
  And I've found a new sweetheart,
  And she treats me so bad.
  I tell you, life is hard
  For any loving man;
  She only shakes my hand
  And my gold ring has fled!

3 I'm foreman now at our refin'ry,
  And I work at the boilers
  By the light of the motor;
  And I'm distilling all
  That sugar-alcohol.
  I guess that you can see
  I know my distillery.

4 Baiana, she only likes wine, boys,
  Yes, and brandy so fine, boys,
  And cognac and such liquor,
  And a cigar in hand
  Of that Lafayette brand,
  And to be gently fanned,
  Good Lord, in hot weather.
    Ah, Baiana,
    Baiana, Lord above!
    Oh, Baiana,
    Baiana, be my love!

A. L. L.

ECUADOR

122 YO SOY INDIECITO

I'm a little Indian

(Canción Religiosa)

Yo soy in - die - ci - to De San Se - bas - tián,

De San Se - bas - tián. En a - yu-nas ven - go Y sin al - mor -

zar, Y sin al - mor - zar, Por cum-plir la vi -

gi - lia De la Na - vi - dad,__ De la Na - vi - dad.

1 Yo soy indiecito
  De San Sebastián. (2)
  En ayunas vengo
  Y sin almorzar, (2)
  Por cumplir la vigilia
  De la Navidad. (2)

1 I'm a little Indian
  From San Sebastian, (2)
  And I have been fasting
  Since the early morn, (2)
  All for to keep my vigil
  Now that Christ is born. (2)

A. L. L.

123 SAN JUANITO

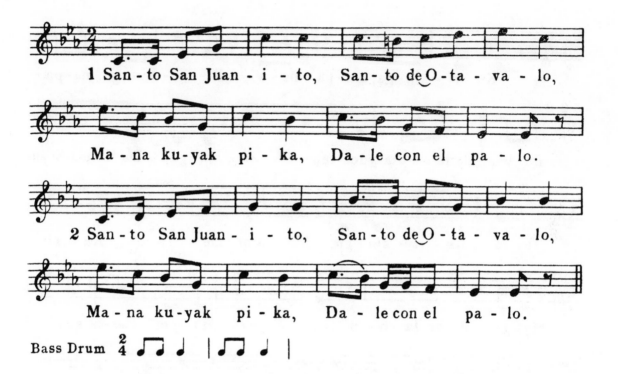

Bass Drum

1 San - to San Juan - i - to, San - to de O - ta - va - lo,

Ma - na ku - yak pi - ka, Da - le con el pa - lo.

2 San - to San Juan - i - to, San - to de O - ta - va - lo,

Ma - na ku - yak pi - ka, Da - le con el pa - lo.

1 Santo San Juanito,
  Santo de Otavalo,
  Mana kuyak pika,
  Dale con el palo.

2 Santo San Juanito,
  Santo de Otavalo,
  Mana kuyak pika,
  Dale con el palo.

1 Holy San Juanito,
  Saint of Otavalo,
  Wake my lazy lover
  With your wand of willow.

2 Holy San Juanito,
  Saint of Otavalo,
  If he doesn't love me,
  Strike him with the willow.

A. L. L.

124 KURIKINGA

(Baile)

Ku - ri - kin - ga, ma - pa - ña - wi,   Ku - ri - kin - ga, ma - pa -

ña - wi,   Da la me - dia vuel - ta,   *Ku - ri - kin - ga,*   Da la vuel - ta en -

te - ra,   *Ku - ri - kin - ga,*   Me - nea que me - ne - a,   *Ku - ri -*

kin - ga,   Be - be la co - pi - ta,   *Ku - ri - kin - ga,*   Has - ta que te

can - ses,   *Ku - ri - kin - ga,*   Ku - ri - kin - ga, ma - pa - ña - wi,   Ku - ri -

kin - ga, ma - pa - ña - wi,   Da la me - dia vuel - ta,   *Ku - ri - kin - ga.*

Drum

ECUADOR

1 Kurikinga, mapañawi,
Kurikinga, mapañawi,
Da la media vuelta,
  Kurikinga,
Da la vuelta entera,
  Kurikinga,
Menea que menea,
  Kurikinga,
Bebe la copita,
  Kurikinga,
Hasta que te canses,
  Kurikinga,
Kurikinga, mapañawi,
Kurikinga, mapañawi,
Da la media vuelta,
  Kurikinga.

1 Kurikinga, two-faced woman,
Kurikinga, two-faced woman,
Swing toward your partner,
  Kurikinga,
Turn and turn about now,
  Kurikinga,
Shake it inside out now,
  Kurikinga,
Drink a little whiskey,
  Kurikinga,
Till it makes you dizzy,
  Kurikinga,
Kurikinga, two-faced woman,
Kurikinga, two-faced woman,
Swing toward your partner,
  Kurikinga.

A. L. L.

Kurikinga: a kind of bird; here the name is applied to a lively woman.

125 PIRUSA

¿Que te pa - re - ce, Pi - ru - sa, Que te pa - re - ce,

Pi - ru - sa, Lo que nos es - tá pa - san - do?

¡Ay, ay, ay, Pi - ru - sa mi - a!

1 ¿Que te parece, Pirusa,
  Que te parece, Pirusa, ⎫ (2)
  Lo que nos está pasando? ⎭
  ¡Ay, ay, ay, Pirusa mia!

1 What is this, O my Pirusa,
  What is this, O my Pirusa? ⎫ (2)
  What is to become of us two? ⎭
  Ay ay ay, my sweet Pirusa!

2 ¡Toma por haber querido, ⎫
  Toma por haber querido, ⎬ (2)
  Y yo por haberte amado! ⎭
  ¡Ay, ay, ay, Pirusa mia!

2 So much the worse that you loved me, ⎫
  So much the worse that you loved me. ⎬ (2)
  So much the better that I loved you. ⎭
  Ay ay ay, my sweet Pirusa!

A. L. L.

PERU

PERU

126 HAKUMAMAI PURISISUN

O dearest mother

(Canción Religiosa)

1 Ha - ku - ma - mai___ pu - ri - si - sun, Hua - hua - llai -
2 Mar - che - mos, ay, ___ ma - dre mí - a, ___ Va - mos en

qui - ta ma - pu - ri - sun, Auc - ca - cu - nacc___
bus - ca de tu hi - jo, Por - que en ma - nos___

ma - quin - pi - ñas Hua - hua - llai - qui - ta ñac ka - ris - can.
e - ne - mi - gas, Ay, pa - de - cien - do el po - bre es - tá.

1 Hakumamai purisisun,
  Huahuallaiquita mapurisun,
  Auccacunacc maquinpiñas
  Huahuallaiquita ñac kariscan.

1 O dearest mother, let us go now.
  Let's go in search of your only son.
  Maybe he lies in enemy hands,
  And, poor young man, we fear he's
                          undone.
                          A. L. L.

2 Marchemos, ay, madre mía,
  Vamos en busca de tu hijo,
  Porque en manos enemigas,
  Ay, padeciendo el pobre está.

224

PERU

127 DIME, LLUVIA, SI YA SE DIVISAN

Tell me, rain

(Huaino)

1 Dime, lluvia, si ya se divisan
  Los cerros, los cerros de mi pueblo,
  Aquellos cerros que debo caminar,
  Y las flores que debo recoger.

1 Oh, tell me, rain, can you see the mountains,
  The peaks, the peaks of my native country,
  Likewise the pass by which I have to travel,
  And the flowers that I have to gather?

A. L. L.

225

128 AL CANTO DE UNA LAGUNA

By the edge of a lagoon

(Huaino)

Al can - to de u - na la - gu - na   He cri - a - do u -

na tro - pa'e vi - cu - ñas.   Al mo - men - to   de mi re - ti -

ra - da   No hay quien me a - com - pa - ñe a llo - rar. __

PERU

1 Al canto de una laguna
  He criado una tropa'e vicuñas. } (2)
  Al momento de mi retirada
  No hay quien me acompañe a llorar. } (2)

1 By the edge of a lagoon, boys,
  There I raised a herd of fine vicuñas. } (2)
  When the moment came for me to
                                leave it, } (2)
  Nobody was there to see me weeping.

A. L. L.

227

129 LA LLUVIA

The Rain

(Huaino)

1 Way, ken-ti-llay ken - ti, Way, tu-ya-llay tu - ya,
1 Oh, pi-ca-flor mí - o, Oh, ca-lan-dria mí - a,

Ri - ma-ku-was kkan-ki Pay mu-nas kkay-man - ta,
Te ha-bías o - cu - pa - do De mi a-mor pa - ra él,

Pay khu-yas kkay-man-ta. 2 Pa-ra-kka pa-ras-ki - an-takk
Oh, pi - ca-flor mí - o. 2 Mas la llu-via va llo-vien-do,

Chi-ri-kka chi-ris-ki - an-takk, Chay - pa chau-pi - chan-pin
Y el frí - o dan-do su frí - o, Al ri-gor de to-do e - so

War - ma ya-nay - ki - kka Mu - nas kka-llay-ki - kka.
Es -tá tu jo-ven a-man-te, Él que mu-cho a - mas.

PERU

1 Way, kentillay kenti,
Way, tuyallay tuya,
Rimakuwas kkanki
Pay munas kkaymanta,
Pay khuyas kkaymanta.

2 Parakka paraskiantakk
Chirikka chiriskiantakk,
Chaypa chaupichanpin
Warma yanaykikka
Munas kkallaykikka.

1 Oh, picaflor mío,
Oh, calandria mía,
Te habías ocupado
De mi amor para él,
Oh, picaflor mío.

2 Más la lluvia va lloviendo,
Y el frío dando su frío,
Al rigor de todo eso
Está tu joven amante,
El que mucho amas.

1 O, my little skylark,
O, my little plover,
You have been so busy
Whistling to my lover,
O, my little plover.

2 The more the rain it does rain, love,
The more the frost it is freezing,
The more the weather is bitter,
The more my darling does please me,
The more the frost is freezing.

A. L. L.

130 EL PUQUITO

The Pigeon

El pu - qui - to que a la pu - na Se ha fu - ga - do e -

stá llo - ran - do, Bus-can-do el le - cho y el ni -

do, Es - tá llo - ran - do.

1 El puquito que a la puna
Se ha fugado está llorando,
Buscando el lecho y el nido,
Está llorando.

2 Nunca has de correr, paloma,
Haciéndote la engreída.
Cuidado que en pueblos ajenos
Tú llores, tú sufres.

3 Y la noche se ha venido
Llena de nubes negras,
Y la nieve lo sacuda
Al pobre puquito.

4 Viéndote en ajenos pueblos,
Mi paloma, mi corazón,
¿Qué padre y qué madre
"Hijo mio" te dirán?

1 A little pigeon came flying
O'er the top of the mountain.
Seeking a bed and a shelter,
There he came lamenting.

2 Do not come this way, my pigeon,
Putting on your airs and graces,
Or else your poor heart may break,
love,
In these distant places.

3 Darkness falls over the mountain,
And the black clouds are gath'ring,
And the poor little cock-pigeon
In the snow is shiv'ring.

4 Here in these outlandish places,
O my pigeon, O my sweetheart,
Who will be father and mother,
Who will call you "My child"?

A. L. L.

BOLIVIA

131 CANTO PARA COSECHAR LA PAPA

(Potato-Gathering Song)

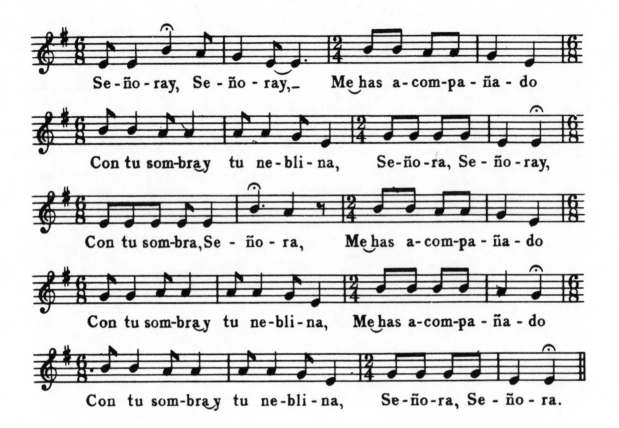

Se-ño-ray, Se-ño-ray,— Me has a-com-pa-ña-do

Con tu som-bray tu ne-bli-na, Se-ño-ra, Se-ño-ray,

Con tu som-bra, Se-ño-ra, Me has a-com-pa-ña-do

Con tu som-bray tu ne-bli-na, Me has a-com-pa-ña-do

Con tu som-bray tu ne-bli-na, Se-ño-ra, Se-ño-ra.

1 Señoray, Señoray,
  Me has acompañado
  Con tu sombra y tu neblina,
  Señora, Señoray,
  Con tu sombra, Señora,
  Me has acompañado
  Con tu sombra y tu neblina, } (2)
  Señora, Señora.

1 Lady, O my Lady,
  You were always with me
  With your mist and with your shadow,
  Lady, O my Lady,
  With your shadow, my Lady,
  You were always with me
  With your mist and with your shadow, } (2)
  Lady, O my Lady.

A. L. L.

132 NAVIDAVA PURI NIHUA

Christmas is here

(Villancico)

Dr. Na-vi-da-va pu-ri ni-hua, Hua-hua-no-ka ku-si-chu ña-my, Ni-ño Je-sus yu-ryt lay-cu A-na-ta-ña la-kis-ta-ny. Ji-cha ka-tus-ta-na-kam-py, Be-len-a-ru-sa ra-ña-ni, -ni, Hua-hua-na-ca.

1 Navidava puri nihua,
Huahuanoka kusichu ñamy,
Niño Jesus yuryt laycu
Anataña lakistany.
Jicha katustanakampy, ⎫ (2)
Belenarusa rañani, ⎭
Huahuanaca.

1 La Navidad ha llegado,
Hijos, nos alegraremos
Porque al Nino Jesús le va ú
A gustar jugar con sus hijos.
Vamos adorarlo, vamos, ⎫ (2)
Vamos adorarlo, vamos, ⎭
Hijos, vamos.

1 Christmas is here with love and light.
Come, O my brothers let's sing all night.
Think of the Holy Babe's delight
To be at play with shepherd boys.
This little child with face so bright ⎫ (2)
Come and adore with heart and voice. ⎭
Come and adore.

A. L .L.

233

133 TAQUIRCAPUSCAIQUI ARI

I'll tell you all about it

(Huaino)

1 Taquircapuscaiqui ari,
Tusurcapusaiqui.
Pitachamunanqui ari,
Pusarcampuscaiqui.

2 Zapatitos bayomanta
Taquitun restares.
Camllamantakis ari
Amistades cachun.

3 Taquircapuscaiqui ari,
Tusurcapusaiqui.
Pitachamunanqui ari,
Pusarcampuscaiqui.

1 Te lo contaré a tí pues
Te lo bailaré.
A quien más quieras así pues
Te la traeré.

2 Calzados bayos para tí,
El taco restares,
De lejos que vean pues
Las amistades.

3 Te lo contaré a tí pues
Te lo bailaré.
A quien más quieras así pues
Te la traeré.

1 I'll tell you all about it, yes,
I'll dance it for you now.
That little girl you love the best
I'm going to steal somehow.

2 Think you're so smart in your tan shoes,
Soon just the heels remain.
All of your friends can see quite clear
You will be fooled again.

3 I'll tell you all about it, yes,
I'll dance it for you now.
That little girl you love the best
I'm going to steal somehow.

A. L. L.

134 HE VENIDO, PALOMITA

My little dove, I cannot stay

(Huanito)

He ve - ni - do, pa - lo - mi - ta, Trai - ga las flo - res que

l'he vol - ver, Só - lo por - que he ve - ni - do.

So - li - ta en los cam-pos ver-des En-can-to de mis a - mo-res.

1 He venido, palomita,
  Traiga las flores que l'he volver,
  Sólo porque he venido.
    Solita en los campos verdes ⎱ (2)
    Encanto de mis amores. ⎰

1 My little dove, I cannot stay,
  Bring me the flowers for I must go.
  I'm here because I chanced this way,
  And now, my love, you've bewitched
                                me, ⎱ (2)
  Standing alone in the meadow. ⎰

A. L. L.

235

CHILE

135 HA NACIDO EN UN PORTAL

He was born in a stall

(Esquinazo al Niño Dios)

1 Ha na - ci - do en un por - tal
tre la mu - la y el buey,

Lle - ni - to de te - la -
El Re - den - tor de las

ra - ñas, Lle - ni - to de te - la - ra - ñas,   En -
al - mas, El Re - den - tor de las   al - mas.

2 Ni - ñi - to lin - do, ay!   Ven pa - ra a - cá.   Tus o - jos

lin - dos, ay!   Me han de sal - var.   Por - que la Vir - gen Ma -

rí - a   Al cie - lo me ha de lle - var,   Al cie - lo me ha de lle - var.

CHILE

1 Ha nacido en un portal
Llenito de telarañas,
Llenito de telarañas,
Entre la mula y el buey,
El Redentor de las almas,
El Redentor de las almas.

2 Niñito lindo, ay!
Ven para acá.
Tus ojos lindos, ay!
Me han de salvar.
Porque la Virgen María
Al cielo me ha de llevar,
Al cielo me ha de llevar.

1 For He was born in a stall,
Spider-webs instead of ribbons,
Spider-webs instead of ribbons,
Between the ox and the ass,
The Redeemer of poor sinners,
The Redeemer of poor sinners.

2 Sweet little baby, now
Come here to me.
I know your pretty eyes
Will set me free.
And then the Virgin Mary
Up to Heaven she will bear me,
Up to Heaven she will bear me.

N. F. and A. L. L.

136 LA PASTORA

The Shepherdess

Al a-ma-ne-cer la a-bro-ra___ A-nun-cian-do el cla-ro

dí-a, ___ Oi-go u-na voz muy so-no-ra___ Al pie de u-na se-rra-

ní-a. ___ Oi-go u-na voz muy so-no-ra___ Al

pie de u-na se-rra-ní-a. ___ Que lin-da la ro-sa, que

lin-do el cla-vel, Más lin-da la da-lia que va a flo-re-cer. No

me mi-res, no me mi-res___ Si tie-nes a quien que-

rer. ___ No me mi-res no me mi-res___ Si

tie-nes a quien que-rer. ___

CHILE

1 Al amanecer la abrora }(2)
  Anunciando el claro día, }(2)
  Oigo una voz muy sonora }(2)
  Al pie de una serranía. }(2)
     Que linda la rosa, que lindo el clavel,
     Más linda la dalia que va a florecer.
     No me mires, no me mires }(2)
     Si tienes a quien querer. }(2)

2 Vi bajar una pastora }(2)
  Toda cubierta de pieles. }(2)
  Para descansar se sienta }(2)
  Debajo de unos laureles. }(2)
  Que linda etc.

3 Leía unos papeles }(2)
  De la historia de su vida. }(2)
  Mientras los iba leyendo
  Se iba quedando dormida (2)
  Debajo de unos laureles.
     Que linda etc.

4 El ganado se le ausenta }(2)
  Y todo se le esparrama. }(2)
  Ella lo busca y lo cuenta, }(2)
  Y queda muy satisfada. }(2)
     Que linda la rosa, que lindo el clavel,
     Más linda la dalia que va a florecer.
     No me mires, no me mires }(2)
     Si tienes a querer. }(2)

1 Just as the dawn sky turned yellow, }(2)
  Announcing that night was ending, }(2)
  I heard a voice clear and mellow }(2)
  All from the hillside descending. }(2)
     How lovely the lilac, how lovely the rose,
     More lovely the dahlia, the fairest that blows.
     Oh, don't look at me, young shepherd, }(2)
     If you have a love of your own. }(2)

2 A shepherdess came down singing, }(2)
  A sheepskin upon her shoulder, }(2)
  And there I spied her sitting }(2)
  All under the spreading laurel. }(2)
     How lovely, etc.

2 And there she sat reading some papers }(2)
  Relating her own life story,
  But that seemed a weary labour,
  For soon fast asleep she had fallen,
  Just as she sat there a-reading
  All under the spreading laurel.
     How lovely, etc.

4 The sheep on their own went straying. }(2)
  The shepherdess woke and lamented. }(2)
  She sought them and found them playing, }(2)
  And so she could rest contented. }(2)
     How lovely the lilac, how lovely the rose,
     More lovely the dahlia, the fairest that blows.
     Oh, don't look at me, young shepherd, }(2)
     If you have a love of your own. }(2)

N. F. and A. L. L.

241

137 DÉJENME PASO QUE VOY

Let me be free

(Cueca)

Guitar

me,   dé-jen-me pa-so que voy,   voy,____ La

vi - da, Y en bus -ca a - gua,   en bus -ca de a-gua se-

re - na,   La vi-da Pa - ra la—,____   pa-

ra la-var-me la   ca - ra,____ Mi   vi - da, Que di-
                                          vi - da, Dé - jen-

cen,_ que di-cen que soy mo - re-na,   La
me,_   dé - jen-me pa-sar que   voy. 2 Aun-

- que soy mo - re - ni - ta, Mi vi - da, No tro-ca-

ra____ Por u - na que tu-vie-ra____ La

CHILE

vi - da, Blan-ca la ca-ra. Aun-que soy mo - re

ni - ta, Mi vi - da, No me tro - ca - ra. Blan-

- ca la ca-ra, sí, _ Mi vi - da, Blan-ca tu pe - na. _ Sí

la a - zu - ce - na es blan - ca, Ay de mí, yo soy mo -

re - na. Sí re - na. Sí, _ la blan-ca a - zu - ce -

- na, Mi vi - da, Yo soy mo - re - na!

1 Déjenme, déjenme paso que voy, (2)
   La vida,
Y en busca agua, en busca de agua serena, } (2)
   La vida,
Para la–, para lavarme la cara,
  Mi vida,
Que dicen, que dicen que soy morena,
   La vida,
Déjenme, déjenme pasar que voy.

1 Let me be, let me be free to go now, (2)
   My darling,
To find water, to find that crystal-clear water, } (2)
   My darling,
For to wash, to wash my face in the morning,
   My darling,
For they say, for they say I'm a dark-skinned girl,
   My darling,
Let me be, let me be free to go now.

243

CHILE

137 Déjenme paso que voy (*continued*)

2 Aunque soy morenita,
　Mi vida,
No trocara
Por una que tuviera
　La vida,
Blanca la cara.
Aunque soy morenita,
　Mi vida,
No me trocara.
Blanca la cara, sí,
　Mi vida,
Blanca tu pena.

3 Sí la azucena es blanca,　　} (2)
　Ay de mí, yo soy morena. }
Sí, la blanca azucena,
　Mi vida,
Yo soy morena!

2 Even though I am dusky,
　My darling,
I wouldn't change,
I wouldn't change with another,
　My darling,
Though she were white.
Although my face is dusky,
　My darling,
I wouldn't change it.
And if her face is white,
　My darling,
White is your sorrow.

3 If the lily is white, love,　　} (2)
　Oh, what then, my face is dusky. }
Ay, the lily is white, and
　My darling,
Oh, my face is dark!

N. F. and A. L. L.

244

138 INGRATO, YA NO ME QUIERES

False lover, now you don't love me

(Tonada)

In - gra - to, ya no me quie-res Co - mo so-lí - as que-

rer-me. Ig - no-ro por que ra - zón_ Pro-cu-ras a - bo-rre-

cer - me. Di-ces que me quie-res Con el al-ma y la

vi - da, Pe-ro me lo jue-gas A las es - con -

di - das. Di-ces que me quie-res Con el co-ra -

zón, Pe-ro me lo jue-gas Cuan-do hay o-ca - sión.

1 Ingrato, ya no me quieres Como solías quererme. Ignoro por que razón Procuras aborrecerme.	1 False lover, now you don't love me, Although you used to adore me, And I don't know what's the reason You find a cause to abhor me.

(continued overleaf)

138 Ingrato, ya no me quieres (*continued*)

Dices que me quieres
Con el alma y la vida,
Pero me lo juegas
A las escondidas.
Dices que me quieres
Con el corazón,
Pero me lo juegas
Cuando hay ocasión.

You say that you love me
With all your life and feeling,
But in fact you tire me
With your double-dealing.
You say that you love me,
And with all your heart,
But in fact you cheat me
Every chance you get.

2 Ingrato, mal pagador,
Atiende lo que te digo;
Que no le pagues tan mal
A quien tanto te ha querido.
Dices que me quieres
Con el alma y la vida,
Pero me lo juegas
A las escondidas.
Dices que me quieres
Con el corazón,
Pero me lo juegas
Cuando hay ocasión.

2 False lover, cheat me no more.
Attend now to what I'm saying;
Don't be so hard on a girl
Who loved you with all her being.
You say that you love me
With all your life and feeling,
But in fact you tire me
With your double-dealing.
You say that you love me,
And with all your heart,
But in fact you cheat me
Every chance you get.

N. F. and A. L. L.

139 EN LA CORDILLERA LLUEVE

It's raining on the mountain

(Cueca)

1 En la cor-di-lle-ra llue-ve, Sí, sí, sí,___ La vi-da, yen la

cor-di-lle-ra llue-ve, Sí, sí, sí,___ La vi-da, yen la

mar es-tá llo-ran-do, Sí, se-ño-ra.___

2 La vi-da, y en la fun-di-cion de a-ce-ro, Sí, sí, sí,___
3 En la puer-ta'e mi ca-sa plan-té u-nas flo-res, Sí, sí, sí,___

La vi-da, ahi ten-go mi a-mor tra-ba - jan-do, Sí, se-ño-ra,___
Pa-ra que se di-vier-tan los fun-di-do-res, Sí, se-ño-ra,___

La vi-da, y en la cor-di-lle-ra llue-ve, Sí, se-ño-ra.___
En la puer-ta'e mi ca-sa plan-té u-nas flo-res, Sí, se-ño-ra.___

4 Los fun-di-do-res, sí fun-dir - ci-to, Sí, sí, sí,___

(continued overleaf)

247

CHILE

139 En la cordillera llueve (*continued*)

Yen mi pe-cho te lle-vo re-tra-ta-di-to, Sí, se-ño-ra.

An-da, mi bien, no llo-res los fun-di-do-res, Sí, sí, sí.

1 En la cordillera llueve,
  Sí, sí, sí,
  La vida, y en la cordillera llueve,
  Sí, sí, sí,
  La vida, y en la mar está llorando,
  Sí, señora.

2 La vida, y en la fundicion de acero,
  Sí, sí, sí,
  La vida, ahi tengo mi amor trabajando,
  Sí, señora,
  La vida, y en la cordillera llueve,
  Sí, señora.

3 En la puerta'e mi casa planté unas flores,
  Sí, sí, sí,
  Para que se diviertan los fundidores,
  Sí, señora,
  En la puerta'e mi casa planté unas flores,
  Sí, señora.

4 Los fundidores, sí, fundircito,
  Sí, sí, sí,
  Y en mi pecho te llevo retratadito,
  Sí, señora,
  Anda, mi bien, no llores los fundidores,
  Sí, sí, sí.

139 En la cordillera llueve (*continued*)

139.

1 Oh, it's raining on the mountain,
   Yes, yes, yes,
   My darling, oh, it's raining on the mountain,
   Yes, yes, yes,
   My darling, and it's weeping out on the sea.
   Yes, señora.

2 My darling, in that smoky old steel foundry,
   Yes, yes, yes,
   My darling, there you'll see my true love working,
   Yes, señora,
   My darling, oh, there's rain on the high mountains,
   Yes, señora.

3 At my door I have planted some red-hot pokers,
   Yes, yes, yes,
   Just to please and amuse all those bold stokers,
   Yes, señora.
   At my door I have planted some fine flowers,
   Yes, señora.

4 Oh, you foundrymen and my foundry sweetheart,
   Yes, yes, yes,
   In my heart I am carrying your dear portrait,
   Yes, señora.
   Go, my love, do not cry for the foundry stokers.
   Yes, yes, yes.

                                        N. F. and A. L. L.

PARAGUAY

140 LA GUAIREÑITA

Es Vi - lla - ri - ca u - na vi - lla her - mo - sa,

De don - de sur - je____ cu - ña - ta - î.____

Lle - na de flo - res____ en sus jar - di - nes,____

Vi - va la pa - tria____ del__ Y - bo - ty!____

Guitar acc.

PARAGUAY

1 Es Villarica una villa hermosa,
  De donde surje cuñata-î.
  Llena de flores en sus jardines,
  Viva la patria del Yboty!

2 Allí yo tengo mi prometida,
  Yporanüégpe na mboyoyai,
  Como el lucero de la mañana
  Que anuncia el bello co'embotá.

1 Oh, Villarica, she is a fine town,
  And she's the cradle of my family.
  She's full of flowers in every garden,
  Long live the homeland of the Yboty!

2 It's there you'll find my own little
                               sweetheart,
  The prettiest girl that ever I spied.
  She's like a star on a summer's morning,
  Heralds a fine day through a cloudy sky.

                                    A. L. L.

253

141 CHE LUCERO AGUAI-Î

The Star called Aguai-i

(Polca Paraguaya)

Guitar acc.
Harp acc.

1 Che____ a - má, se - ño - rá,____ Nda - yu - húi____

____ nde yo - gua - há;____

Pei - na - mó____ nde tî - vî - tá____

Nde re - sa o - ya - yá yá - yái,____

____ Î - vá - ga - ré____ o - ñe - pin - tá.____ 2 Che____

Ni íu - ce - ro____

____ no - mba - yo - yái.____ 3 A - ra - mo - ro - ti po - tî,____ O - pai -

- té mbo - e - saî;____

Che lu - ce - ro A - gua - i - î____

____ O - mbo - yo - yá - va Kua - ra - hî.____ 4 Ne - po - rá - ha ne - po -

ti, Re - he - sa - pé ha - re - mi - mbé;____ O - páo - ye____

____ ro - kî ro - kî,____ Che lu - ce - ro A - gua - i - î.____

254

PARAGUAY

1 Che amá, señorá,
 Ndayuhúi nde yoguahá;
 Peinamó nde tîvîtá
 Îvágaré oñepintá.

2 Che amá, señorá,
 Ndayuhúi nde yoguahá;
 Nde resa oyayá yáyái,
 Ni lucero nombayoyái.

3 Aramoroti potî,
 Opaité mboesaî;
 Che lucero Aguai-î
 Omboyoyáva Kuarahî.

4 Neporáha, nepoti,
 Rehesapé haremimbé;
 Opáoye rokî rokî,
 Che lucero Aguai-î.

1 O my beloved sweetheart,
 You are handsome beyond compare,
 With your eyebrows like the new moon
 That in heaven shines so fair.

2 O my beloved sweetheart,
 You are handsome beyond compare,
 And your eyes they are so bright, love,
 They outshine the morning star.

3 And your whiteness like a blossom
 Seems to dazzle my poor eyes.
 Like the star they call Aguai-i,
 You're gone just as the sun does rise.

4 You are beautiful as charming,
 And you sparkle and you shine,
 But elusive as a firefly
 Or the star called Aguai-i.

A. L. L.

ARGENTINA

142 YO NO CANTO POR CANTAR

I don't sing just to be heard

(Baguala salteña)

1 Yo no can - to por can - tar, Ni por te-ner bue - na voz. __

Drum

Can-to pa - ra e-char fue - ra Las pe-nas del co-ra - zón.

2 No sé que tie-nen las pe - nas Que no me quie-ren de - jar. __

Hoy me se - pa - ro de e-llas, Ma-ña-na me vuel-ve'al-can - zar.

ARGENTINA

1 Yo no canto por cantar,
  Ni por tener buena voz.
  Canto para echar fuera
  Las penas del corazón.

2 No sé que tienen las penas
  Que no me quieren dejar.
  Hoy me separo de ellas,
  Mañana me vuelve' alcanzar.

1 I don't sing just to be heard,
  Nor is my voice all that fine.
  I'm singing so that my troubles
  May leave this heart of mine.

2 I don't know why my troubles
  Try so hard to remain.
  Today I manage to leave them,
  Tomorrow they meet me again.

A. L. L.

143 DESPIERTA MI PALOMITA

Awake, my beloved

(Carnavalito)

1 Des-pier-ta mi pa-lo-mi-ta, Cu-cu-
lí ma-dru-ga-do-ra. Yo to-ca-ré mi cha-
ran-go. A-le-gre es-tá, La Pas-cua vie-ne Y se a-ca-ba-rá.

2 Car-na-val, car-na-va-li-to, Car-na-val, car-na-va-
li-to, Ju-ran que me han de ma-tar,—Me han de matar. La Pas-cua vie-ne, Cho-li-tay.

ARGENTINA

1 Despierta mi palomita,
  Cuculí madrugadora.
  Yo tocaré mi charango.
    Alegre está,
    La Pascua viene,
    Y se acabará.

2   Carnaval, carnavalito, (2)
    Juran que me han de matar,
    Me han de matar.
    La Pascua viene,
    Cholitay.

3 En la puerta de tu casa,
  Cuculí madrugadora,
  Se ha'i componer el fandango
    Alegre está,
    La Pascua viene,
    Y se acabará.

4   Carnaval, carnavalito, (2)
    Juran que me han de matar,
    Me han de matar.
    La Pascua viene
    Cholitay.

1 Awake, awake, my beloved.
  Rise up now, dove of the morning.
  You hear me play my charango.
    It's holiday,
    For Easter's here and
    Soon will be gone.

2   Carnaval, carnavalito, (2)
    They swear that they have to kill me,
    They have to kill,
    For Easter's here now,
    Cholita!

3 Right at the door of your house, love,
  – Rise up now, dove of the morning!
  They've started up a fandango.
    It's holiday,
    For Easter's here and
    Soon will be gone.

4   Carnaval, carnavalito, (2)
    They swear that they have to kill me.
    They have to kill,
    For Easter's here now,
    Cholita!
                                    A. L. L.

Charango: a small guitar-like instrument, having a body made of armadillo-shell.

Cholita: an affectionate name, meaning 'little half-caste girl'.

261

144 AHORA VOY A CANTARLES

All the night long I'll be singing

(Carnaval de Tilcara)

1 A ho-ra voy a can - tar - les Has-ta que a-pun-te el lu - ce - ro.
2 En el lu-gar don-de vi - vo Tris-te pa-dez-co, llo-ran-do.

Los car-na-va - les ya vie-nen Des-de la ci - ma del ce - rro.
A es-te ba-rrio he ve - ni - do A di-ver-tir - me can-tan-do.

1 Ahora voy a cantarles
Hasta que apunte el lucero.
Los carnavales ya vienen
Desde la cima del cerro.

2 En el lugar donde vivo
Triste padezco, llorando.
A este barrio he venido
A divertirme cantando.

3 ¡Todos, toditos, arriba!
¡El carnaval ha llegado!
Domingo, lunes y martes,
Tres días y se acabo.

1 All the night long I'll be singing
Right till the daylight is dawning.
Carnival dancers are coming
Down from the hills in the morning.

2 Plenty of trouble and sorrow
There in the place where I'm living.
Now I've come down to this village
To drive off sorrow with singing.

3 Rise up now, all you good people,
The carnival is arriving.
Sunday and Monday and Tuesday,
Three days and then it's all over.

V. K. and A. L. L.

145 CANSADO ESTOY DE VIVIR

I'm weary of living

(Vidala)

Guitar and Drum

Can - sa - do es - toy de vi - vir, ___ A - diós, vi - di - ta,
Más bien mo - rir es - pe - ran - do, A - diós, vi - di - ta,

La vi - da que es - toy vi - vien - do, Tal - vez no vuel - va ja - más.
Que no vi - vir pa - de - cien - do, Tal - vez no vuel - va ja - más.

1 Cansado estoy de vivir, } (2)
  Adiós, vidita,
  La vida que estoy viviendo,
    Talvez no vuelva jamás.
  Más bien morir esperando, } (2)
  Adiós, vidita,
  Que no vivir padeciendo,
    Talvez no vuelva jamás.

2 Todos me desean la muerte, } (2)
  Adiós, vidita,
  Pena tienen que ande vivo,
    Talvez no vuelva jamás.
  Como si yo les quitara, } (2)
  Adiós, vidita,
  Prendas que de ellos han sido,
    Talvez no vuelva jamás.

1 Well now, I'm weary of living, } (2)
  Adios, vidita,
  This kind of life that I lead here,
    Maybe I'll never come back.
  Better to perish in hope, } (2)
  Adios, vidita,
  Than go on living and suffer,
    Maybe I'll never come back.

2 Everyone wishes me dead here, } (2)
  Adios, vidita,
  Everyone's vexed that I'm living,
    Maybe I'll never come back.
  I swear you'd think that I'd taken, } (2)
  Adios, vidita,
  Jewels that used to be theirs, love,
    Maybe I'll never come back.

A. L. L.

146 UNA PALOMITA

A little dove

(Vidalita)

1 Una palomita,
   Vidalitá,
  Que yo la crié,
  Quando tuvo alitas,
   Vidalitá,
  Se voló y se fué.

2 Todos son despojos,
   Vidalitá,
  Desde que se fué.
  No hay rama en el monte,
   Vidalitá,
  Que florida esté.

1 Oh, a little white dove,
   Vidalita,
  That I once did rear,
  Soon as it had wings, love,
   Vidalita,
  Flew away from here.

2 All around is ruin,
   Vidalita,
  Since she went away.
  Not a tree on the mountain,
   Vidalita,
  Ever blooms again.

A. L. L.

147 PUES QUE ES LO QUE ME DICES

Since all that you've been saying

(Chacarera)

1 Pues que es lo que me dices
Que me lo dijeron dos,
Para secarme los ojos
Cuando me acuerdo de vos.

2 El arbol que se seca
No vuelve a florecer,
Como el amor olvidado
Que no vuelve a aparecer.

3 Chacarera, chacarera,
Chacarera, un verde ser;
Si no fueras tan tirana
No me hicieras padecer.

1 Since all that you've been saying
I know to be surely true,
It's better I dry my eyes, love,
Whene'er I remember you.

2 The tree that grows in dry country
Can't flower for want of rain,
And nor can a love forgotten
Ever come to life again.

3 Chacarera, chacarera,
Chacarera, young and green,
If you weren't so domineering,
Well, you wouldn't cause such pain.

V. K. and A. L. L.

148 DICEN QUE NO ME QUIERE

They say that you don't love me

(Gato)

Guitar (arpeggio)   Di -

cen que no   me   quie - re_   Pe - ro bien hai - ga.   Di -

cen que no   me   quie - re_   Pe - ro bien hai - ga.   La

des - pe - di - da es cor - ta,_ La au - sen - cia lar - ga.   La

des - pe - di - da es cor - ta,_ La au - sen - cia lar - ga.

La au - sen - cia lar - ga, sí._   Ay, que no pue - do

Ol - vi - dar el ca - mi - no_ Del Rí - o Ne - gro.

ARGENTINA

1 Dicen que no me quiere⎱ (2)
  Pero bien haiga.   ⎰
  La despedida es corta, ⎱ (2)
  La ausencia larga.   ⎰
  La ausencia larga, sí.
  Ay, que no puedo
  Olvidar el camino
  Del Río Negro.

2 El naranjo en el cerro ⎱ (2)
  No da naranjas,   ⎰
  Pero da los azahares ⎱ (2)
  De la esperanza.   ⎰
  De la esperanza, sí,
  Y así decía
  Cuándo tendrán alivio
  Las penas mías.

1 They say that you don't love me.
  Indeed, you do wrong.
  The parting is soon over,
  But absence is long.
  But absence is long, love,
  Ay, though I must go,
  I'll not forget the road, love,
  To Rio Negro.

2 The tree upon the mountain,
  The fair orange-tree,
  Yields no fruit, yet its blossom
  Brings sweet hope to me.
  Brings sweet hope to me, love,
  That fortune will mend.
  It comforts me, saying
  My sorrow will end.

V. K.

149 DICEN QUE LAS HELADAS

They say the frost in winter

(Cueca)

Di-cen que las he-la - das   Se-can los yu - yos.

A-sí me voy se-can - do, mi vi-da, De a-mo-res tu - yos.

1 Dicen que las heladas
   Secan los yuyos.
   Así me voy secando, mi vida, ⎫ (2)
   De amores tuyos.   ⎭

2 Tengo un palacio aquí,
   Otro en Mendoza,
   Otra en la Villa Nueva, mi vida, ⎫ (2)
   De Santa Rosa.   ⎭

1 They say the frost in winter
   Withers both grass and tree,
   And like the grass in winter, beloved, ⎫ (2)
   I perish without thee.   ⎭

2 I have a nearby palace
   And one in Mendoza,
   And one in Villanueva, beloved, ⎫ (2)
   In Santa Rosa.   ⎭

ARGENTINA

3 De Santa Rosa, sí,
   Digo en deveras,
   Que si no fuera cierto, mi vida,
   No lo dijera.
   Cierto lloro y me muero, mi vida,
   Porque te quiero.

4 Para qué quiero, vida,
   Si no la logro,
   Si me muero, hago falta, mi vida,⎫ (2)
   Si vivo, estorbo.   ⎭

5 Si vivo, estorbo, sí,
   Así te digo,
   Que castigarme quieres, mi vida,⎫ (2)
   Con el olvido.   ⎭

6 Con el olvido, sí,
   Te castigara.
   Yo había sido el primero, mi vida,
   Que me olvidara.
   Ahora sí que cuando, mi vida,
   Vivo penando.

3 In Santa Rosa, ay,
   A palace there as well.
   I would not tell you false, my beloved;
   This is the truth I tell,
   For sure I weep and die, beloved;
   I love you too well.

4 Why do I love, beloved,
   If I cannot enjoy?
   If I should die, you'll miss me, beloved.⎫ (2)
   Alive, your peace I destroy.   ⎭

5 Destroy your peace, I tell you,
   And of this I am sure:
   You want to punish me, O beloved,⎫ (2)
   And think of me no more.   ⎭

6 I too will punish you, love,
   Showing indifference.
   I was your first lover, beloved,
   Now you drive me hence.
   'Gainst pain of unhappy love, beloved,
   There is no defence.

V. K.

URUGUAY

150 LA TERRIBLE INMENSIDAD

Dark and Immense are these plains

(Estilo)

1 La te-rri-ble in-men-si-dad__ En mi des-car-ga sus-pi -
2 Con mi des-ti - no lu-chan-do Y sin en-con-trar bo-nan -

ra.
za.

Los pla-ce-res son men-ti - ra; Só-lo la pe-na es ver - dad.__
Su-frien-do es-tá mi es-pe-ran-za. Di-me, for-tu-na, has-ta cuán -

URUGUAY

1 La terrible inmensidad
  En mi descarga suspira.
  Los placeres son mentira;
  Sólo la pena es verdad.

2 Con mi destino luchando
  Y sin encontrar bonanza.
  Sufriendo está mi esperanza.
  Dime, fortuna, hasta cuándo.
    Esa tu sed de vida
    Me tiene siempre penando.

1 Dark and immense are these plains,
  And they cause me for to sigh.
  All the world's pleasures are lies;
  The only true thing is pain.

2 Everything seems to go wrong
  The more I struggle with fate.
  Here I grieve early and late.
  Fortune, come tell me: How long?
    And your keen thirst for life
    Only makes sorrow more strong.

                              A. L. L.

INDEX OF TUNES

No.

105 Adorar al niño *182*
144 Ahora voy a cantarles *262*
85 Al amanecer del día *147*
128 Al canto de una laguna *226*
110 Amalia Rosa *192*
94 Anansi, play for Ma Dogoma *166*
77 ¡Ay! tituy *130*

55 (The) Babe of Bethlehem *88*
37 Black is the colour *66*
3 Blanche comme la neige *6*
20 Bold Wolfe *36*
13 (The) Bonny Banks of the
Virgie O *26*
48 (The) Buffalo Skinners *78*
108 (La) Burriquita *188*

70 Cajeme *116*
145 Cansado estoy de vivir *263*
131 Canto para Cosechar la Papa *232*
98 Cap'n Baker *170*
113 (El) Carite *196*
102 (La) Cartagena *177*
141 Che lucero Aguai-î *254*
41 (The) Chickens they are crowing *70*
121 Colônia, usina Catende *214*
116 Como pode vivir o peixe *204*
106 (La) Corona *184*
66 (El) Cura no va a la iglesia *108*

118 Da Bahia me mandaram *208*
96 Dandy man, oh *168*
34 Daniel Monroe *62*
12 Dans les chantiers nous
hivernerons *24*
7 Dans les Haubans *14*
36 (The) Dear Companion *65*
137 Déjenme paso que voy *242*
143 Despierta mi palomita *260*
149 Dicen que las heladas *268*
148 Dicen que no me quiere *266*
80 Dig my grave long an' narrow *138*

No.

127 Dime, lluvia, si ya se divisan *225*
63 Dry Bones *100*
49 (The) Dying Cowboy *80*

99 Emma *171*
139 En la cordillera llueve *247*
10 En roulant ma boule *20*
39 Every night when the sun goes in *68*

17 (The) False Young Man *30*
73 Flores de Mimé *122*
88 For Atti Daï *152*

140 (La) Guaireñita *252*
29 (The) Gallows Tree *54*
57 Gideon's Band *92*
62 Go down, Death *98*
52 (The) Grey Goose *85*
16 (The) Gypsy Laddie *29*

135 Ha nacido en un portal *238*
126 Hakumamai purisisun *224*
87 Hay aquí, madre, un jardín *149*
134 He venido, palomita *235*
78 Hojita de guarumal *134*
27 (The) House Carpenter *50*

59 I'll hear the trumpet sound *95*
138 Ingrato, ya no me quieres *245*
2 Isabeau s'y promène *4*

33 Jackie Frazier *60*
8 J'ai cueilli la belle rose *16*
89 Jéorico *154*
91 John Thomas *160*

124 Kurikinga *220*

9 Là-haut sur ces montagnes *18*
58 Lay dis body down *94*
46 (The) Lazy Farmer *75*
97 Leggo me han' *169*

275

No.

11 Lisette *22*
26 Little Matthy Groves *48*
44 Liza Anne *73*
129 (La) Lluvia *228*
31 Locks and Bolts *58*
6 (Le) Long de la mer jolie *12*
14 (The) Lover's Ghost *27*
24 (The) Lumber Camp Song *42*
30 (The) Low-Down Lonesome Low *56*
54 Lynchburg Town *87*

18 (The) Maid on the Shore *32*
19 (The) Maiden's Lament *34*
67 Malhaya la cocina *111*
45 Mamma's gone to the mail boat *74*
109 (El) Mampulorio *190*
23 Mary Ann *40*
82 Má Teodora *142*
68 (El) Matrimonio Desigual *112*
103 Mi Compadre Mono *178*
79 Mi Pollera *135*
65 Miren cuántas luces *106*
28 Mr Woodbury's Courtship *52*
53 Mule on the Mount *86*

71 Nací en la cumbre *118*
115 (La) Nau *Catarineta 202*
132 Navidava puri nihua *233*
32 (The) Nightingale *59*

90 Oh, Selina *158*
15 Oh, who is at my bedroom window? *28*
69 (Las) Olas de la laguna *114*
93 Once I was a trav'ller *163*
47 Ox-Driving Song *76*

101 (El) Pajarillo *176*
75 Papanulan *126*
86 Para los caficultores *148*
136 (La) Pastora *240*
35 (The) Pinery Boy *64*
125 Pirusa *222*
40 Pretty Saro *69*
147 Pues que es lo que me dices *265*
130 (El) Puquito *230*
61 Put John on the islan' *97*

No.

4 Quand j'étais chez mon père *8*
114 Que el cantar tiene sentido *198*

50 Red Iron Ore *82*
1 Renaud *2*

5 (La) Sainte Vierge aux Cheveux Pendants *10*
42 Sally Buck *71*
123 San Juanito *219*
112 Sanguéo *195*
74 (El) Sapo *124*
111 Se fué volando *194*
64 Señora Santa Ana *104*
51 (A) Shanty-Man's Life *84*
22 She's like the swallow *39*
21 (The) Stormy Scenes of Winter *38*
43 Swing a lady round *72*

133 Taquircapuscaiqui ari *234*
60 Tell all the world, John *96*
117 Tenho um vestido novo *206*
150 (La) Terrible inmensidad *272*
92 Three acre o' coffee *162*
56 Tone the bell easy *90*
107 Tono de Velorio de Cruz *186*
76 (El) Toro Pinto *128*
119 Triste vida é do marujo *210*

146 Una palomita *264*

84 Vamos a hacer un ajiaco *146*
72 Vamos a la mar *119*
104 Van cantando por la sierra *180*
120 Vem cá, Cabeleira *212*

38 When first to this country a stranger I came *67*
25 (The) Wife of Usher's Well *46*
95 Wind'ard Car'line *167*
81 (The) Wind blow east *139*

142 Yo no canto por cantar *258*
83 Yo quisiera vivir en la Habana *144*
122 Yo soy indiecito *218*

100 (El) Zancudo *174*

276